"In the ever-changing, fast-paced, and turbulent world we live in, *The ABC's of Effective Leadership* is a timeless gift that one can cherish for a lifetime. I highly recommend this book to all aspiring to lead with their heart and spirit."

R. Murali Krishna, M.D.
President, INTEGRIS Mental Health, Inc.
James L. Hall, Jr., Center for Mind, Body, and Spirit
Oklahoma City, Oklahoma

"I have interviewed some of the major leaders of current times, including President Bush, Colin Powell, Zig Ziglar, Michael Dell, and Wally Amos, for both print media and/or our syndicated radio show, 'Business of Success.' However, when I heard Dr. Tom Massey share some of his leadership concepts on our radio show and reviewed his new book on leadership, I knew he was sharing a very special gift on how you can get better at discovering and developing your own personal strengths. Use this book as a roadmap for plotting a course to accomplish great things in your life!"

Alan Rothman
Radio host, the Business Talk Radio Network
Los Angeles

"To thrive in this age of empowerment, companies must understand developing the capacity of the people and the organization. Leaders are feeling overwhelmed and uncertain. Dr. Tom Massey has authored a book on leadership that encapsulates the challenges and responsibilities of the position and makes it seem as simple as our ABCs. His book can be a new beginning in leadership or a breath of fresh air to get refocused on your purpose in leading your organization."

Dottie Caldwell, Ph.D.
Director of Professional Development,
Oklahoma Commission for Teacher Preparation

"*The ABC's of Effective Leadership* is a practical, no-nonsense tool for success at all levels of an organization. The stories, applications, and affirmations 'raise the bar' for leadership handbooks, as they bring focus to our inner selves, both professionally and personally."

William R. Boyd
Senior Vice President, Boyd Gaming Corporation
Las Vegas, Nevada

Gotta Minute

W9-CKC-364

The
ABC's
of
Effective
Leadership

FOR KATE,
BEST WISHES FOR
SUCCESS IN
LEADERSHIP!
Tom Massey

Managing from the Heart

by Tom Massey, Ph.D.

Robert D. Reed Publishers • San Francisco, California

Robert D. Reed Publishers
750 La Playa Street, Suite 647
San Francisco, CA 94121
Phone: 650/994-6570 • Fax: 650/994-6579
E-mail: 4bobreed@msn.com
Web site: www.rdrpublishers.com

Designed and typeset by Katherine Hyde
Cover designed by Julia A. Gaskill

ISBN 1-885003-77-3

Library of Congress Control Number 2001088128

Produced and Printed in the United States of America

This book is dedicated to my family and friends with great joy, appreciation, and love.

Foreword

*I*n October 2001, Dr. Tom Massey delivered a wonderful presentation—"Winning the Battle over Worry"—in Oklahoma City, sponsored by the James L. Hall, Jr., Center for Mind, Body, and Spirit. I was truly impressed with the simple and eloquent style of his presentation, which conveyed a very powerful message along with practical tips for winning the battle over worry.

The ABC's of Effective Leadership is an excellent guide for anyone who is leading others or who aspires to be a leader, with its powerful stories, practical tips, and touching affirmations. The reader is gently guided into grasping the true essence of leadership. Tom has uniquely conveyed his very powerful insights in simple, yet articulate language that touches one's heart and stimulates creative energy. This book has the potential to transform the reader into a wise and effective leader by giving him or her the skills to mobilize the infinite, dormant, creative energy that is waiting to be tapped into within every human being.

In the ever-changing, fast-paced, and turbulent world we live in, *The ABC's of Effective Leadership* is a timeless gift that one can cherish for a lifetime. I highly recommend this book to all aspiring to lead with their heart and spirit.

R. Murali Krishna, M.D.
President, INTEGRIS Mental Health, Inc.
James L. Hall, Jr., Center for Mind, Body, and Spirit
Oklahoma City, Oklahoma

Contents

Introduction 1

1 Acknowledgment 2

2 Adversity 4

3 Become... 6

4 Break Away 8

5 Champion a Cause 10

6 Climb 12

7 Delegate 14

8 Do Unto Others 16

9 Ease into a New Position 18

10 Equality 20

11 Find Fulfillment and Purpose 22

12 Focus Your Attention 24

13 Give Continuous Feedback 26

14 Great Work Environments 28

15 Haste Makes Waste 30

16 Hire the Best 32

17 Information Overload 34

18 Integrity 36

19 Job Security 38

20 Jumpstart Creativity 40

21 Keep Aligned with Your Vision 42

22 Know When... 44

23 Leave Your Comfort Zone 46

24 Let Go of the Outcome 48

25 Manage by Mingling   50

26 Manage Conflict Creatively   52

27 New Directions   54

28 Never Underestimate...   56

29 Online   58

30 Ordinary People   60

31 Perception Shapes Reality   62

32 Play To Win   64

33 Quality Training   66

34 Quit Demotivating   68

35 Respond Instead of Reacting 70

36 Risks   72

37 Skip the Comparison   74

38 Speak   76

39 Take Charge   78

40 Throw Your Heart Over the Bar 80

41 Unstring Your Bow   82

42 Use Every Setback   84

43 Vary Your Leadership Style   86

44 Visionary Leadership   88

45 Who before What   90

46 Write It Down   92

47 eXcellence   94

48 eXpect Delayed Gratification 96

49 Yield the Power   98

50 Your Hill To Die For?   100

51 Zero In on Your Health   102

52 Zoom In...   104

Introduction

*T*he *ABC's of Effective Leadership* provides insights and practical tools that work for improving performance, accelerating process development, and succeeding in a world that is constantly changing. It will help leaders bring out the best in people, whether they work in corporations, educational institutions, government offices, small businesses, churches, or other not-for-profit groups.

What is an effective leader? One who stands out from the crowd, challenging the status quo and doing the unexpected in search of new directions. They are catalysts for change by pushing the envelope and challenging others to think "outside the box."

Effective leaders are trustworthy individuals who lead by example and deliver on their promises. They treat people with respect and fairness. They get things done efficiently through influence and are able to convey a compelling vision of the future.

If you are ready to bring changes in attitude, creativity, buy-in, and commitment to your business, this book will benefit you. It follows a simple ABC format. Each letter of the alphabet is represented by two words or phrases. Each word or phrase, fifty-two in all, is presented as a weekly tip for effective leadership. Each weekly tip includes a brief narrative or story, a practical application, and a daily affirmation.

I suggest that you take your time and use this book as a weekly resource for managing from the heart. Whether you choose to breeze through it in an hour, or move through it slowly, you will find it to be a transformational guide for effective leadership.

Tom Massey

Acknowledgment

Everyone wants to feel important!

*M*any years ago, when my son was a young boy, he and I regularly took walks together in the woods. Being a typically rambunctious boy, he never walked beside me. Rather, he would constantly run ahead, then stop and wait for me to catch up. One day on one of our walks, he ran ahead of me, then crawled up on a big rock and sat down to rest. When I caught up with him, he said, "Daddy, let's just sit on this rock and talk for a while." I climbed up on the rock, sat beside him, and said, "Okay. What do you want to talk about?" He responded with utmost seriousness, "I don't care, just as long as it's *important!*"

So it is with each of us. We all have an innate need to feel important to those around us. We want to count for something. Effective leaders garner the greatest amount of dedication and effort by acknowledging and validating people. When you make people feel as though who they are and what they have to say is important, they will give every ounce of strength to perform what you request. As a famous field general once observed, "Men will die for ribbons."

Acknowledging others costs very little in terms of tangible items, such as money. But it will cost one of your most priceless resources: *time.* Your time and attention are the most valuable gifts you will share with people, but **the return on your investment will be worth it!**

Application

How are you doing at acknowledging the people around you? One of the best ways to make others feel important is to really listen to them. Actively and intently engage others by making eye contact and giving full attention to what they say. Instead of quietly formulating what you are going to say next, simply suspend those thoughts and intently listen to them. It is also a good practice to ask questions and mirror back what they said by repeating what you heard. This decreases the risk of mis-understanding by giving them a chance to clarify whether or not they communicated what they intended.

Another way to acknowledge people is to solicit their input and feed-back about upcoming decisions that affect them and the organization. If you include people in the decision-making process, they will take a greater amount of ownership for their personal contribution to the suc-cess of the organization and be more adaptable to change.

Affirmation

I acknowledge others and make them feel important to me by giving them the gifts of time and attention.

Adversity

2

Struggle gives birth to progress!

*O*ne day a man and his young daughter were looking at a butterfly's cocoon when they noticed a small opening on the side. They sat and watched for over an hour as the butterfly struggled to force its little body through that tiny hole. After a while it seemed to stop making any progress and appeared as if it had gotten as far as it could go. The little girl pleaded with her father to do something, so the man took his fingernail clippers and snipped off the remaining bit of the cocoon. The butterfly then emerged easily, but its body was swollen, and its wings were small and shriveled. They continued to watch the butterfly in hopes that its wings would expand enough to support its body. That didn't happen. The butterfly crawled around with a swollen body and shriveled wings, and eventually died, without ever being able to fly.

Though the man acted out of kindness, he did not understand that the restriction of the cocoon and the struggle required for the butterfly to break free were actually Nature's way of forcing fluid from the butterfly's body into its wings so that it would be ready for flight, once it achieved its freedom from the cocoon. Sometimes struggle is exactly what we need to strengthen us so that we can overcome life's obstacles and fly.

Adversity elicits talents and strengths in you that may have otherwise lain dormant. The greater the challenge, the higher you are likely to soar. The American man of letters Thomas Paine observed, "The harder the conflict, the more glorious the triumph. What we obtain too cheaply, we esteem too lightly; it is dearness only that gives everything its value. I love the man that can smile in trouble, one that can gather strength from distress and grow brave by reflection. 'Tis the business of little minds to shrink; but he whose heart is firm, and whose conscience approves his conduct, will pursue his principles unto death." **Effective leaders view adversity as opportunity in work clothes.**

Application

Do you view adversity as a problem or an opportunity? Don't become masochistic and create unnecessary struggles for yourself, but do begin to look at challenges in your life as growth opportunities. When adversity arises, ask yourself, "What is the lesson in this?" The best way out is through. Rather than always taking the easy way out, face it head on and move directly through the conflict. As you do, you'll become stronger, smarter, and wiser in the process.

As a leader, you will inevitably encounter those who are facing personal challenges. You may have the inclination to jump in and help them out of a jam, but remember the butterfly's struggle to freedom. Sometimes it is better to be a cheerleader who stands by offering words of encouragement than a rescuer who steps in and cuts away the cocoon. The bumps and bruises that people receive from falling down will often serve to strengthen and enable them to overcome life's obstacles. Allow others the opportunity to grow as you do yourself.

Affirmation

I become better each day in every way by treating adversity in my life and others' as opportunities to grow in strength and wisdom.

Become

3

...The change you wish to see!

A mother once took her daughter to a great teacher to ask him for help in getting the girl to quit eating sugar. The mother pleaded, "Master, please command my daughter to stop eating sugar." The old sage instructed the mother to bring her daughter back to him in one month and he would do as she requested. Exactly one month later, the woman returned with her daughter as she was told. At that moment, the teacher waved his finger in the girl's face and commanded her, "Stop eating sugar!"

The mother was a little put off that she had to wait a month and make a second trip to the man in order for her daughter to hear those three short words. Why couldn't he have spoken them on the first trip? When she inquired about this later, the teacher told her, "I could not command your daughter to do something I had not done myself. I stopped eating sugar one month ago. So now I can tell her to do the same."

As a leader you will be called upon to facilitate changes that affect people and situations. Change is inevitable. Without it there can be no growth, and without growth we cease to actively live. Effective leaders walk their own talk. Mahatma Gandhi said, "You must be the change you wish to see in the world." **Do not ask of people what you are unwilling to do yourself!**

Application

Your credibility as a leader relies much more on what you do than on what you say. The best way to facilitate change in those around you is to lead by example and become the change you wish to see. Others will be much more inspired to follow your lead.

Tom Massey

The next time you are called upon to initiate change in others, ask yourself, "What do I need to first change about myself to see this take place in them?" When you take this approach to leadership, you will be much more effective, with greater compassion and appreciation for your constituents. And you'll be pleasantly surprised to see that, when you create change in yourself, people in your life will do likewise. Who you are and what you do influences others.

Are you currently having difficulty with a particular person? Next to financial concerns, strained relationships are the most common source of stress. Can you really change the person you experience difficulty with? Not unless he or she wants to and is willing to do it him- or herself. But you can change yourself. Become the change you want to see in others.

Affirmation

I model effective leadership by becoming the change that I want to see in the world.

Break Away

...From old thought patterns!

*I*talian physicist and astronomer Galileo Galilei was born near Pisa, on February 15, 1564. Throughout his life he became a symbol of "outside the box" thinking. In the field of astronomy, Galileo perfected the use of the telescope in the observation and discovery of sunspots, lunar mountains and valleys, the four largest satellites of Jupiter, and the phases of Venus. In physics, he discovered the laws of falling bodies and the motions of projectiles.

Geniuses are often met with opposition. The philosophy professors of his day scorned Galileo's discoveries because Aristotle had held that only perfectly spherical bodies could exist in the heavens and that nothing new could ever appear there. Galileo was also attacked because of a book he published in 1612 on his discoveries in physics.

His staunchest critic was the Roman Catholic Church, which subjected his books to censorship and instructed him to no longer hold or defend the concept that the earth moves. During the Inquisition in 1632, the Cardinal of the Church summoned Galileo to Rome to stand trial for "suspicion of heresy." The next year he was convicted of the charge and was sentenced to life imprisonment, which was later commuted to permanent house arrest. His books were ordered burned, and the sentence against him was to be read publicly in every university. Galileo eventually lost his eyesight and died at Arcetri, near Florence, on January 8, 1642.

In 1979, Pope John Paul II ordered an investigation into the condemnation of Galileo, and a full exoneration followed as the papal commission acknowledged the Vatican's error and issued a complete reversal of the charges. Galileo's lifelong struggle to free creative thinking and scientific inquiry from philosophical and theological restrictions transcends science. He was willing to break away from old thought patterns at the cost of his reputation and ultimately of his physical freedom. However, his personal stand against societal norms opened the door for others, like Sir Isaac Newton, to carry the torch of great scientific discovery.

Effective leaders have the courage to think "outside the box," even when they meet resistance from those who don't. Albert Einstein said, "Great spirits have always encountered violent opposition from mediocre minds." **Expand your mind and free your spirit to create!**

Application

Do you ever ask yourself the question, "Who are the Galileos of today?" Are you a leader who cultivates an environment that is fertile for new ideas? Become an advocate for creative thinking by allowing yourself and others to move outside the box of societal norms. Think about how you can harness the energy of imagination to discover and create something wonderfully new. Applaud others for innovative ideas, even when they don't get off the ground. Remember, the Wright brothers had more than a few crashes before they became airborne. You live in the most exciting time in history. There are vast opportunities to launch into the adventure of new discovery. What are you waiting for?

Affirmation

I am free to expand and encourage others to think "outside the box" as we continually reinvent and create a better world.

Champion a Cause

5

Believe in something bigger than yourself!

*A*s a young man in the early 1940s, Nelson Mandela was doggedly determined to make a difference in the freedom struggle of his people in South Africa. He became politically active and was elected in 1942 to the African National Conference (ANC), where he impressed his peers with disciplined work and consistent effort in battling racism.

Mandela opened the first black legal firm in his country in 1952. During the entire decade of the 1950s, he was the target of various forms of repression. He was banned from practicing law, arrested, and imprisoned. He was forced to live apart from his family, moving from place to place to evade detection by government informers. He adopted numerous disguises, sometimes dressing as a common laborer and other times as a chauffeur.

In 1962, Mandela was given a five-year jail sentence for inciting his countrymen to strike against apartheid and racial injustice. While serving his first sentence, he was brought up again on trumped-up charges and given life imprisonment. He spent nearly three decades in prison, most of which was in solitary confinement to keep him from influencing the other prisoners and guards. He was offered freedom several times under the condition that he renounce the activities of the ANC, but Mandela refused to compromise the principles he embraced.

He finally gained release from prison in February, 1990, at the age of 72. By that time, Nelson Mandela had become a worldwide symbol of the triumph of the human spirit over man's inhumanity to man. He won the Nobel Peace Prize in 1993 and accepted it on behalf of all South Africans who suffered and sacrificed to bring peace to their land. On May 10, 1994, he was inaugurated as the first democratically elected State President of South Africa and served in that office until June, 1999.

A journalist once asked Mandela how he withstood the torture of almost three decades imprisoned in solitary confinement. His response was, "Oh, that wasn't torture, that was preparation. Those years prepared me to lead my country."

Effective leaders leave lasting legacies in the world by championing causes bigger than themselves. **He who has done his best for his own time has lived for all times.**

Application

What causes are you championing? Is there something that you feel passionate enough about to risk everything for? There is sustaining strength in passion. Regardless of your age or the obstacles you face, if you have good "why" you can overcome any "what." And when you become impassioned, others will follow. People will be drawn to you like a magnet. Courage will be echoed in your voice and hope will be reflected in your eyes. You will make a difference when you champion a cause bigger than yourself.

Affirmation

I am passionately committed to a cause bigger than myself as I work each day to create a better world.

Climb

6

...Your own ladder of success!

*C*hris loved every aspect of sports, from playing to coaching. And he was very good at it. He would have liked to go into coaching full time, but his dad agreed to help pay for Chris's college expenses on the condition that he major in engineering. Consequently, Chris felt obliged to struggle through semester after semester, for eight long years, attending engineering school. He had to retake many courses because of poor grades and academic probation.

One day I asked Chris why he continued to subject himself to something he obviously wasn't good at and didn't want to do. He recounted, rather wistfully, how his dad had dreamed of him becoming an engineer and he just hated to let his dad down. I asked, "Chris, which do you think would really make your father happy, you becoming a mediocre engineer or an outstanding coach?"

Sadly, he continued this path and finally graduated from engineering school with a 2.2 grade point average (GPA), the lowest average one could have and still graduate. After graduation, Chris discovered that 2.2 GPA engineers are not in great demand in the job market. His search for an engineering position was futile. But Chris had bittersweet feelings about his situation. On one hand, he was frustrated and disappointed that he couldn't find an engineering job, yet at the same time, he was a little relieved because deep inside he didn't want to be an engineer anyway.

Chris found a job driving a delivery truck for a parcel service. Now he spends his days delivering parcels and dreaming of being a coach. Can you relate to this story? Have you found yourself climbing the ladder of success, only to discover that the ladder was leaning against the wrong wall? Effective leaders lead by example. And one of the best examples you can provide is to **do the work you love.**

Application

Did someone else write the script for your career path? Or are you currently doing work that you chose because of your interests, natural talents, and enthusiasm? Those are the characteristics that will propel you to do something great with your life. Without those characteristics, you're likely to find yourself plodding along in a mundane daily routine of mediocrity.

As a leader, you cannot give away that which you do not have. Inspire others by your authenticity and willingness to climb your own ladder to success. Create opportunities for people to discover their real talents and what they love to do. This will empower them to climb their own ladders to success, making the greatest contribution to your organization and to the world.

Affirmation

I am climbing my own ladder to success based on my talents and passion, and I encourage others to do the same.

Delegate

7

Work smart, not hard!

*J*ohn complained that he had more work than he could complete, even in a twelve-hour workday. He worked late day after day, while his constituents and associates left the office each day by 5:30 P.M. He knew the custodial night crew on a first-name basis. John was beginning to experience a sense of desperation and burnout. His job had become a tremendous burden, and he was considering looking for a different one.

Sound familiar? Are you working hard, not smart? If so, you could benefit from learning better delegation skills.

Many of us were exposed to delegation as children when we heard our mother tell the babysitter: "This is what you do if . . . if there is any trouble call me at . . ." Everyone knows about it, but few actually understand how to use delegation effectively.

The fear of loss of control is one of the main reasons leaders are hesitant to relinquish authority to others. But this need not be the case. If you teach constituents, by example and full disclosure, to apply the same criteria that you do in decision-making and task management, they will exercise control on your behalf. Furthermore, since you can't be in several places at once, they will experience many more situations and opportunities to exercise that control more diversely and in a more timely manner than you could exercise it by yourself. In engineering terms: If maintaining control is your utmost concern, then you should distribute the control mechanisms to enable parallel and autonomous processing.

Effective leaders use delegation as a powerful tool to empower individuals to reach their fullest potential. When used successfully, delegation will free you to rise above the tree line to gain a broader perspective for visionary leadership. If you were able to free up one hour a day by delegating some of the tasks that you currently perform yourself, how would you use that time to increase your effectiveness as a leader? **Begin today!**

Application

Consider the question, "What do I delegate and what do I do myself?" Take a long-term view on this issue. To be an effective leader, delegate as much as possible to assist others in rising to higher levels of performance and to free your own time for long-range visioning. The following suggestions provide a "how-to" approach to delegation:

1. Develop a clear understanding of what needs to be done and who should do it, then clearly communicate it to the individual receiving the delegated task.
2. Establish why the task is important and how it fits into the big picture of your organization, and explain it to the delegate.
3. Define the results you are looking for, what standards you expect, what deadlines need to be met, and any consequences for not achieving those results.
4. Ensure that the delegate has both the authority and the resources to accomplish the task.
5. Explain how you will support the delegate in completing the task, and contact him periodically to evaluate how the assignment is going and whether he needs additional assistance.

Affirmation

I model effective leadership by regularly practicing excellent delegation skills.

Do Unto Others

...As *they* would have you do!

*D*uring the Vietnam War, one of the army units in Saigon had a diminutive South Vietnamese cook named Lee, who helped prepare their meals. The soldiers in the unit teased Lee mercilessly and played practical jokes on him almost daily. He became very timid and cautious around the men because of the ridicule he received. The men began to feel badly about their abusive behavior and promised one day not to tease or play any more jokes on Lee.

Lee looked at them with surprise when they shared the news with him. "No more *tease?*" he said. "No more tease," they declared. He grinned widely and exclaimed, "Then no more *spit* in soup!"

During a corporate managers' training session recently, the topic of customer service came up. I asked the group, "What's the worst thing that happens when your customers' needs aren't met?" They concurred that the customers usually leave, grumbling about the bad service, taking their business elsewhere. I then asked the same question about employees' needs. The consensus was pretty much the same: disgruntled employees, like customers, leave and find jobs elsewhere. I agreed, but reminded them that something worse often happens when employees' needs aren't met. Some of them stay with the organization and start spitting in the soup!

Effective leaders know that their most valuable customers are internal—the people within the organization. Those are the customers that will make or break you the quickest. They can be your organization's greatest ambassadors or most difficult antagonists.

Many of us were taught from early childhood to follow the Golden Rule: *Do unto others as you would have them do unto you.* The problem with that philosophy is the assumption that everyone wants to be treated as you do. It's akin to saying, "One size fits all." And we all know that's not true. A better rule to follow is the Platinum Rule: *Do unto others as they would have you do unto them.* That's how to truly meet the needs of others. **When in doubt: ask!**

Application

Do you practice the Platinum Rule? Are the people within your organization contributing to its long-term success, or are they spitting in the soup?

People are your greatest resource, your cultural capital. As an effective leader, much of your time will be spent investing in this capital by helping to meet people's needs. How else will you know others' needs except by asking? Ask open-ended questions that cannot be answered with a simple "yes" or "no." Open-ended questions are powerful because they stimulate thinking, encourage greater discussion, and reduce the likelihood of taking definite positions on issues not yet thoroughly discussed.

Build rapport with others by listening and observing. Listen to the words they say and observe their face, body position, and movements. Paraphrase what has been said to demonstrate understanding and express feedback based on what you have observed. You are communicating all the time. Are you communicating warmth, or are you sending a message of indifference? Whatever you send, you will receive.

Affirmation

I practice the Platinum Rule each day as I treat others as they want to be treated.

Ease into a
New Position

9

Learn the lay of the land first!

*L*ee accepted a position as director for the computing services department of a Midwestern university. He was a retired military officer, accustomed to running a tight ship. However, this new ship was anything but tight. People were used to working flexible hours—coming in late, working late. The work environment was casual, but the quality of service was reasonably high. Often programmers and technical consultants would work late into the evening assisting students and faculty on computer-related projects.

Lee was a stickler for structure. He issued an immediate directive that everyone must be in the office by 8:00 each morning and take 45 minutes for lunch beginning at noon each day. Time was his utmost concern and people would be accountable for it, by God.

Chaos ensued. People started grumbling about the new "bean-counter" for a boss. The quality of service deteriorated because attitudes began to shift. Employees were no longer willing to go the extra mile to help customers. Everyone packed up and left each evening at five o'clock, regardless of the workload.

Lee found himself in a big mess. The final straw came when the top four programmers resigned to take other jobs. These near-genius employees were the glue that held the department together—definitely not the people that Lee wanted to run off. They took with them a great deal of knowledge about the intricacies of the computer's operating system, along with some of the source code for programs they had developed for university computer users. If you know anything about computer programming, you know how invaluable and irreplaceable source code is. Losing it can be catastrophic.

The situation went from bad to worse. After directors from other departments repeatedly filed complaints about the loss of service quality, Lee was requested to resign his position and leave the university—hopefully much wiser than when he came.

Effective leaders ease into new positions of authority. They learn the lay of the land before plowing it up for replanting. They form alliances with the real players and informal leaders that hold the place together. **Effective leaders seek first to understand others before enforcing their own agenda.**

Application

Are you currently in a new position, or looking at changing positions? Expect it to take somewhere between sixty and ninety days to acclimate to your new environment. Be willing to listen and observe without making immediate judgments. Become familiar with day-to-day operations to gain an understanding of the tasks people perform. Identify and make alliances with the key players, the informal leaders and those who contribute the most to the success of the organization. Find out what your constituents (both internal and external) think. What's working? What's not?

Include key people in the planning stages of any organizational changes you want to implement. First, get buy-in, then engage them as allies to influence others. Don't try to change too many things too quickly. For major changes, draft a phased plan with plateaus built in to allow people time to rest and catch their breath before making the climb to the next level.

Affirmation

I seek first to understand and solicit the support of others before initiating organizational changes.

Equality

Lead with a democratic spirit!

*A*braham Lincoln went to Gettysburg, Pennsylvania, on November 19, 1863, to present a speech for the dedication of the Gettysburg National Cemetery, honoring those who died in the Civil War battle that had taken place there earlier that year. It has been said that Lincoln wrote the speech on the back of an envelope during the train ride to the dedication ceremony. His entire discourse lasted two minutes, receiving very little applause.

Lincoln's short speech followed a two-hour oration by Edward Everett, the main speaker at the event and one of the most famous speakers of the time. In the newspaper reports of the dedication ceremonies, Everett's remarks were highly lauded and prominently printed on the front page, while the words of Lincoln were relegated to an inside page. Everett, however, was greatly moved by the simple and sincere eloquence of Lincoln. He sent the president the following note on the day after the dedication: "I wish that I could flatter myself that I had come as near to the central idea of the occasion in two hours as you did in two minutes."

Although Lincoln felt at the time that his speech was a failure because of the lack of public response, the Gettysburg Address is universally recognized today as a classic model of the noblest kind of oratory, and one of the most moving expressions of the democratic spirit ever uttered. This great champion of democracy succinctly captured his deepest personal conviction with these words: "Fourscore and seven years ago, our fathers brought forth on this continent a new nation, conceived in liberty, and dedicated to the proposition that *all men are created equal.*"

Effective leaders understand the essence of those words spoken by Lincoln. Indeed, all people are created equal. Regardless of a person's position on the organizational chart, everyone plays an integral part in the success of an organization. The sack boy in a grocery store is as important as the store manager. The night clerk at a hotel plays as vital a role as the general manager.

Acknowledge and honor each person's contribution to the success of your organization.

Application

Do you embrace people at all levels within your organization? Do you foster loyalty by offering a democratic approach to decision making? By treating people with a sense of equality, you will create stronger alliances that play a vital role in your long-term success. Pave the path of the future by relating to others, not from a position of self-interest, but from a position of what is good for all.

Affirmation

I create strategic alliances by embracing each person as an equal partner in the pursuit of happiness and success.

Find Fulfillment and Purpose

11

Become a servant leader!

*R*ecently I received a call from a man who is an executive for a successful telecommunications firm. He said that he had to make a major decision about the future direction of his life, and asked if we could get together to discuss it. When we met, the man told me, "My company is thriving. I am financially secure. I have good health. I have a wonderful family and am well respected in the community. I suppose that I should be happy and contented, but it just seems that there should be more to life than this."

Despite great worldly success, our lives may lack a sense of fulfillment or purpose. The Dalai Lama, who has been the spiritual and political leader of his country for over forty years, was once asked the question: "What is the purpose of life?" He responded, "The reason we are on this planet is to serve one another. That is the entire reason for our existence."

Effective leaders possess a deep sense of commitment to excellence, achievement, quality, and growth, coupled with compassion, humility, gratitude, and service.

If you want to experience more purpose and fulfillment, focus on helping others. Lead through serving. **Help to bring out the best in people, and you'll find the best in yourself!**

Application

Is something lacking in your life? If so, focus on potential areas of service. Begin by genuinely listening to others and empathizing with their needs and concerns. Give what you wish to receive. As you help others self-actualize, you'll discover self-actualization taking place in your own life. Follow these four action strategies:

Tom Massey

1. **Focus** on meeting the needs of others.
2. **Develop** employees to bring out the best in them.
3. **Coach** others and encourage their self-expression.
4. **Facilitate** personal growth in everyone you work with.

As a leader, seek to persuade others rather than pull rank. Think beyond the day-to-day concerns to the larger vision. Exercise foresight through viewing outcomes based on past lessons, realities of the present, and consequences of the future. Become the most optimistic person you know and believe in the intrinsic value of individuals, as you nurture personal and professional growth in others. Build a stronger work environment by promoting opportunities for working together, while respecting the dignity of individuals to provide service to the world.

Affirmation

I find meaning and purpose through service as I seek mutual fulfillment and growth with others in my life.

Focus Your Attention 12

Don't look where you don't want to go!

S ome years ago, Kathy, a good friend and training partner, took me rappelling outside Birmingham, Alabama. I had never been rappelling and, quite frankly, was more than a little fearful of heights. The palms of my hands and my feet began to sweat profusely every time I even thought about standing in high places. She told me that this should be a very empowering experience and assured me that I was completely safe. "You have nothing to fear but fear itself," she said. "Yeah, right," I thought.

The place Kathy chose was a gorgeous state park with beautiful bluffs about 100 feet high from the top to the valley floor below. She took me to her favorite spot, which was a place where the rocks jutted out about 20 feet at the top, so when we stood at the top all we could see was the ground about 100 feet below. I crept up to the edge of the cliff and peered downward. The sweat began to pour. With fear and trepidation, I imagined myself plummeting and crashing into the valley floor below. A huge lump filled my throat as I moaned, "That's a loooong way down." She calmly replied, "Don't look where you don't want to go."

Effective leaders keep their sights fixed on where they want to go. What you place your attention on expands into your life. If you focus on what you want, that's what you will attract. If you focus on the things you don't want, guess what appears over and over? This is simply a variation of the sowing and reaping principle. By the law of the Farmer, you'll reap exactly what you sow—so don't plant what you don't want to grow.

You possess the power to create. Dwell on thoughts or circumstances that serve you and the people in your organization. Instead of seeking what you don't want, **look for the positive in all people and situations.**

Application

During the Vietnam War era, a group asked Mother Teresa to come to Washington, D.C., to participate in a demonstration against the war. They shared with her how they hoped to attract over a million people to this event, and her presence would be a very large draw. She declined, saying, "I will not participate in a demonstration *against* war, but if you have one *for* peace, let me know, I'll be there." In her vast wisdom, Mother Teresa realized that the things we are against weaken us, while the things we're for strengthen us.

What has your attention? Are you looking to the sky with anticipation or to the ground with dread? Don't look where you don't want to go. You will be most effective as a leader by maximizing strengths and minimizing weaknesses. Focus on what your people do well. Become a raving fan and cheer them onward. Lead by example and keep your sights on what you want.

Affirmation

I constantly look where I want to go and become strengthened by keeping my mind focused in the right direction.

Give Continuous Feedback

13

...To promote peak performance and growth!

*H*ow does the snake eat an elephant?" the old swami asked his students. "One tiny bite at a time," was the answer.

The annual performance review can sometimes seem like trying to eat an elephant in one sitting. The manager sits down with the employee and proceeds to itemize every issue and fault that has arisen in the past year. For the person on the receiving end, this can feel like opening a box of hate mail. Her attitude turns to defensiveness, and her ability to listen or learn becomes drastically diminished.

Annual performance reviews mostly serve to fill employees' files. A much better way to offer feedback is with a regular lunch date or chat over coffee. People thrive on continuous feedback, especially casual gestures, comments, interactions, or actions of an informal nature. Formal feedback tends to heighten anxiety levels, which decreases the brain's ability to internalize information received.

Continuous feedback will decrease risks of miscommunication. In the absence of feedback, people begin to hunt for messages, even to the point of creating them from assumptions based on the thinnest of clues. This often leads to misunderstandings, hurt feelings, and unnecessary conflict.

Effective leaders utilize continuous feedback as a valuable tool for influencing others' performances. It lies at the heart of personal and professional growth. Be sensitive to what you communicate. While words are important, the vast majority of the message you deliver is beyond the words you speak. People read body language, tone of voice, and pace of speech. Be clear about the message that you convey to people and **help others "raise the bar" of personal performance by offering positive, continuous feedback.**

Application

Do you give continuous, constructive feedback to others? Are you a catalyst for growth or an obstacle? To improve your feedback skills, practice the following tips:

1. Organize your thoughts before giving feedback in order to pinpoint the real issues.
2. Become more aware of what you are communicating through body language, tone of voice, and pace of speech.
3. Set a personal goal to provide others with immediate feedback that is positive and beneficial.
4. Make sure that your intentions are clearly understood and stay sensitive to how others receive the message.
5. Encourage feedback from others to help you grow as a leader, and be willing to receive it without developing a posture of defense.

Affirmation

I am a catalyst for growth in others by offering continuous feedback that is positive and practical.

Great Work Environments

14

Money's not everything!

*D*uring their preparation to write *Love 'Em or Lose 'Em: Getting Good People to Stay,* authors Beverly Kaye and Sharon Jordan-Evans performed two years of research, asking over three thousand people in diverse positions and industries to reflect upon the top reasons they stay with an organization. The top ten reasons, in order of popularity and frequency, were:

1. Personal career growth, learning, and development
2. Exciting and challenging work
3. Meaningful work—making a difference and a contribution
4. Great people
5. Being part of a team
6. Good boss
7. Recognition for work well done
8. Fun on the job
9. Autonomy—sense of control over my work
10. Flexibility, including work hours and dress code

Notice that money is not on the list. Sure, money matters—if you don't compensate people fairly, the talented people will leave. But contrary to what most managers believe, money is not the most important factor for employee retention or job satisfaction. People want an opportunity to grow and perform meaningful, challenging work in an environment that provides teamwork, fun, recognition, and flexibility. Effective leaders understand that people want and need to be cared about. That is a wise investment, considering it costs sometimes double their annual salary to replace key people.

The U.S. Bureau of Labor Statistics projects by the year 2006 there will be ten million more jobs than there will be people in the workforce to fill them. Economic growth will be limited in the next decade simply because there won't be enough people to meet the job demand.

The message is clear: The era of expendable workers is drawing to a close. Talented people are scarce, and becoming scarcer as the new millennium unfolds. **Do your best to keep good people by creating an environment for growth!**

Application

What kind of a work environment are you creating? Do you support and encourage personal growth and enrichment? Are you friendly and validating to others? Do you display passion, yet flexibility in dealing with day-to-day issues? Are you a trustworthy leader and mentor who acts with compassion and sensitivity?

Tune in to people. Share information and show respect by keeping them in the loop on decision making. Create opportunities for meaningful, challenging job assignments driven by people's enthusiasm and interest. When you take care of others, they will take care of you.

Affirmation

I am creating a great work environment that offers meaningful work, growth opportunities, and a chance to be a part of a high-performing team.

Haste Makes Waste 15

Don't judge on looks alone!

A woman in a faded gingham dress and her husband, dressed in a homespun threadbare suit, stepped off the train in Cambridge, Massachusetts, and walked timidly without an appointment into the president's outer office. The secretary quickly discerned that such backwoods, country hicks had no business at Harvard University.

"We want to see the president," the man said softly. The secretary frowned and snapped back, "He'll be busy all day." "We'll wait," the woman replied.

The secretary ignored them for hours, hoping that the couple would become discouraged and go away. They didn't. The secretary finally grew frustrated and decided to disturb the president, even though it was a chore she regretted to do. "Maybe if they just see you for a few minutes, they'll leave," she told him. He sighed in exasperation and nodded.

The stern-faced president strutted out to meet the couple, thinking that someone of his importance obviously didn't have the time to spend with the likes of people dressed in gingham dresses and homespun suits.

The woman told him, "We had a son who attended Harvard for one year. He loved Harvard. He was happy here, but he was accidentally killed a year ago, and we would like to erect a memorial to him, somewhere on campus."

Instead of being touched, the president was shocked at their audacity. "Madam," he said gruffly, "We can't put up a statue for every person who attended Harvard and died. If we did, this place would look like a cemetery."

"Oh, no," she explained, "We don't want to erect a statue. We thought we would like to give a building to Harvard." The president rolled his eyes. He glanced at the gingham dress and homespun suit, then

Tom Massey

exclaimed, "A building? Do you have any earthly idea how much a building costs? We have over seven-and-a-half million dollars in the physical plant at Harvard."

For a moment the woman was silent. The president was pleased, thinking he could get rid of them now. She finally turned to her husband and said quietly, "Is that all it costs to start a university? Why don't we just start our own?" Her husband nodded.

The president's face wilted in bewilderment as Mr. and Mrs. Leland Stanford walked away, traveling to Palo Alto, California, where they established the university that bears their name—a memorial to a son that Harvard no longer cared about.

Hasty decisions made on looks alone can result in the loss of golden opportunities. Effective leaders learn to remain unmoved by the way things appear on the surface. They have the patience to wait until the mud settles and the waters clear, as they **allow all situations to unfold in the most beneficial manner.**

Application

How do you judge the appearances of people and situations? Do you look beyond the surface level to see what lies at the heart of the matter? The next time you have the inclination to make a rash judgment or decision, take a deep breath, pause, and listen. Things are not always as they appear. Priceless treasures often come from the most unexpected sources. Be patient and keep an open mind. Life's greatest gifts may be dressed in a gingham dress or a homespun suit.

Affirmation

I suspend all judgment and patiently allow all situations to transpire for good.

Hire the Best

16

...And you'll attract good people!

*A*lice, a divorced mother of two, was caught in the middle of a massive downsizing in the corporation for which she had worked for over a decade. During her tenure with this company, she had attended night classes at the local university, earning both undergraduate and graduate level degrees. Additionally, she learned a variety of useful skills on the job and worked her way into a management position. Because of her diligence and hard work, Alice became one of the most qualified employees in her position, but now she found herself looking for work in a saturated job market.

Initially, Alice was optimistic because she had worked hard at attaining a repertoire of job skills and becoming college-educated. She put together a résumé that highlighted her assets and began to search for open positions. Unfortunately, she found that management positions such as the one she held with her former employer were in small demand. Instead, most of the openings were entry-level. "No problem," Alice thought. She had started at the bottom before and worked up, so she could do it again.

Her first few interviews were discouraging and frustrating. At the conclusion of each, she heard those monotonous words, "You are overqualified for this position." Even though Alice assured them that she was enthusiastic about joining the organization and would love to get the chance to prove herself, each interviewer expressed that he felt she would get bored with the job or become dissatisfied and leave quickly.

Out of desperation, Alice omitted her graduate degree and several skills from her résumé, thinking that downplaying her qualifications would help her to land a job more quickly. She put them back after I convinced her that she wouldn't do herself or the world any favors by playing small. I assured her that someone would indeed appreciate her skills and hard work.

Effective leaders have the courage to hire the best people they can. They don't buy into the lame argument that overqualified people will only use the company or the position as a stepping-stone to something bigger and better. That type of thinking is motivated by scarcity consciousness. The best way to attract good people to your organization is to **develop a reputation for hiring the best for every job!**

Application

What kind of people do you seek to hire? Do you hesitate when considering someone who has more qualifications than the job requires? Are you uncomfortable with job candidates who seem smarter than you? Don't be. Hire the smartest, most qualified people you can find, then give them the responsibility and the resources to do the best job they can. Look for more than skill-set. Hire for attitude, character, and enthusiasm. So what if they leave? Replace them with the smartest, most qualified people you can find. The quality of your organization depends on the quality of the individuals you attract. Hire the best!

Affirmation

I hire the top qualified person I can get for every position.

Information Overload

17

Get a handle on it!

*T*he amount of information that is available today is overwhelming. A single issue of a daily *New York Times* contains more information than the average person in the early 1800s would have seen in a lifetime. Americans are exposed to almost ten times as many advertisements today as they were thirty years ago. It is estimated that the amount of printed information doubles every five years. And the Internet has made more information accessible than most of us ever dreamed possible. It is simply mind-boggling!

Pitney-Bowes, the manufacturer of postage meters, recently conducted a study which concluded that the average office worker sends and receives thirty-six e-mail messages, thirty-six pieces of regular mail, fifty-two phone messages, and fourteen faxes a day. It is estimated that the average worker spends a cumulative total of one month out of her work year sifting through all the correspondence.

The bombardment of statistics, communications, and advertisements can eventually take its toll on a person. It can cause physical ailments such as headaches and stomach pain. It can lead to stress-induced memory problems and the inability to focus or pay attention. Ultimately, information overload can hurt your ability to perform.

Effective leaders know the importance of screening out unneeded information. They focus on what is pertinent at the moment. If you want to be productive and efficient, get a handle on information overload. **Focus on things that matter most.**

Application

Deliberately collect information based on what you need. For instance, select only that which helps you to plan, prepare, create, clarify values, empower others, and build productive partnerships. Instead of trying to learn everything, focus in on specific details that are pertinent to your goals. Learn to recognize information that is credible, especially when using the Internet. Much of what is available on the World Wide Web comes from unreliable sources.

Develop productive habits for dealing with information. Set aside particular times each day to handle paperwork and respond to e-mail. Handle routine tasks in order of priority without procrastination. Focus on what is important at the moment and leave everything else until you have time to deal with it. Discard what you don't need. If you can survive without it, toss it. By prioritizing and simplifying, you will enhance your quality of work along with your state of well-being.

Encourage constituents to simplify and prioritize, as well. Be sensitive to overwhelming them with information and countless meetings that take up excessive amounts of their work time and diminish their productivity.

Affirmation

I am focusing specifically on the information that is important and essential for my personal and professional growth.

Integrity

18

...What we do when we think no one is looking!

A young man and woman were headed to a nearby lake to spend some quiet moments alone. They decided that a picnic would be nice, so they stopped to pick up some fried chicken on the way out of town. The man went in and ordered a box of chicken, while the woman waited in the car. The person who took his order boxed up the chicken and set it down on the counter beside an identical box that contained the money and receipts from the previous workday, which the manager had prepared to take to the bank for deposit. After the man paid his bill, the person at the counter mistakenly handed him the box of money, instead of the box that contained the chicken.

On the way to the lake, the couple opened the box and discovered the mistake. The man immediately turned the car around and headed back to the restaurant to return the box of money. The manager of the store greeted him with elation. He told the man how relieved he was that the money had been returned, as he went on and on about the man's honesty. The manager said that he had a friend who was a reporter for the local newspaper and he wanted to call his friend to write a news story lauding the man's good deed.

The man thanked the manager for the offer, but told him that he did not want to go to the trouble of reporting the story. The manager kept insisting, refusing to take "no" for an answer. Finally, the man blurted out, "Sir, you cannot report this to the newspaper. I'm a married man and the woman I'm with is not my wife!"

This is not a moral judgment about anyone's behavior. I share this story simply to make this point: Honesty and integrity don't always ride on the same bus. Effective leaders live and walk with integrity, even when no one is looking. They are completely trustworthy. Their character reveals a

Tom Massey

solid foundation of impeccability upon which honor and influence are built. **No legacy is so rich as one molded by integrity.**

Application

Are you living in integrity? Do you think you're the only one who knows? What internal rules or codes of conduct have you set for yourself? Are you honoring those standards, even when you think no one is looking? As a leader, you must face the fact that people are watching you from every direction. Choose to lead by example and live in integrity. As Will Rogers once said, "Live your life in such a way that you wouldn't be afraid to sell the family parrot to the town gossip."

Affirmation

I am committed to live with integrity at all times, especially when no one else is watching.

Job Security 19

Where's the loyalty?

A friend, who works for a major corporation that just let thousands of people go in a major downsizing, told me: "This has been a terrible experience—so many people that I've known and worked with for years were demoted, booted out, or transferred. It has been difficult for everyone here. I still have my job, but I'll never feel the same about this company.

"I've been here over twenty years," she said, "and over that time we were given the sense that as long as we did a decent job, the company would stand by us. Then all of a sudden we were told, 'No one is guaranteed a job anymore.'"

There is a growing unease that no one's job is safe anymore, even in a thriving economy. A major telecommunications company announced its intention to lay off forty thousand workers the same year it reported a record five-billion–dollar profit. National recruiting firms report that more than half of callers making inquiries about jobs are still employed—but are fearful of losing their jobs. And a recent poll reported that one-third of Americans fear that someone in their household will lose his or her job.

One worker commented to me, "There's no way to give your loyalty to a company anymore and expect it to be returned. You're expected to be part of a team, yet be ready to move on upon short notice. So each person is becoming his own shop within the company."

Effective leaders understand that long-term organizational success depends on shared loyalties and mutual benefit with employees. Regardless of the services or products your company produces, people are your greatest asset. You don't owe people a career or a living, but keep in mind that reengineering and streamlining your organization is about more than reducing head counts and throwing people out of work. Resist this national tidal wave and refuse to engage in the churning of people. As my grandfather said, **"Dance with those that brought you!"**

Application

Many of the baby-boom–era workers were taught that education and technical skills were permanent tickets to success. In today's labor market, we see that success takes more than intellectual excellence or technical prowess. You can invest in people by emphasizing that they work on internal qualities, as well as specific technical skills. Here are some traits that will increase worker effectiveness and marketability:

1. Listening and oral communication skills
2. Optimism and adaptability to setbacks and obstacles
3. Self-control, confidence, motivation, and a sense of pride in achieving goals
4. Social skills, cooperation, and teamwork
5. Enthusiasm and desire to make a contribution

Affirmation

I garner loyalty by valuing others and investing in internal qualities that benefit both the organization and individuals.

Jumpstart Creativity

20

Make work fun!

*C*reativity and fun walk hand in hand, according to a study conducted by a team of psychologists at the University of Maryland. Researchers selected two groups of college students, who were shown two different videos, then given a range of creative problems to solve. The first group viewed a five-minute film clip of comical bloopers lifted from various sitcoms and weekly television shows. The second group of students watched a math video that was very dry and technical.

As expected, the students in the first group, who had been laughing before the test, fared better at creative problem-solving than the group who watched the math video. But researchers were astonished that the members of the first group proved to be 300 to 500 percent more efficient at problem-solving than their counterparts.

You can increase the power of creativity in your organization drastically by permitting people to laugh and have fun before tackling problems. Where there is fun, there is enthusiasm. Where there is enthusiasm, there is energy. And in the presence of energy, creativity abounds.

Consider how often you laugh on a typical day. Laugh experts tell us that prepubescent children laugh on the average of 110 times per day. As the years pass, the laughter quotient begins to drop drastically, and by their mid-forties, adults typically laugh an average of only eleven times per day. Where did our smiles go between childhood and adulthood?

Understand that all laughter is not the same when it comes to creativity. Laughing *with* someone is much different from laughing *at* someone. The first is a tool for enhancing creativity, while the second produces the opposite effect. Laughing with others is nourishing, supportive, and confidence-building. It brings people closer together in a team spirit of cohesiveness and harmony.

Effective leaders know that **fun and creativity are inextricably linked with success!**

Application

Stimulate creativity in your workplace by fun-filling the environment with conversation pieces, toys, and other objects that provoke light-heartedness and laughter. You don't have to be dead serious to be productive. In fact, whoever started that rumor is probably dead . . . seriously.

Try leading your next team meeting wearing a beanie-cap with a propeller on top. Incite others to laugh with you, and with one another. By doing so you will generate an environment where people feel self-confident and relaxed. Your workplace will then become fertile ground for the growth of creativity and inspiration.

Generate high energy through promoting friendly competition between work teams. By making a game of it, you will engage people's competitive nature to turn in a winning job performance. When work is fun, people stay at it longer with much greater enthusiasm.

Affirmation

I jumpstart creativity and enthusiasm each day by making work fun and competitive in a friendly way.

Keep Aligned with Your Vision

21

...And move toward it each day!

*T*he Tibetans have an epic poem about a mythical hero named Gesar, who was chosen by the gods for a great mission. His purpose was to overcome four evil kings who were intent on destroying the faith of the people. Gesar overthrew the first king, but was sidetracked when he became infatuated with the king's wife. He settled into luxury with her, becoming satiated and losing sight of his great mission. After six years, the gods came to Gesar and vividly reminded him to get on with his work.

Many of us are like Gesar. We were chosen to accomplish great things, but have become distracted, settling into comfortable old habits that keep us stuck in velvet ruts. Each day turns out to be another postponement of the mission we are here to fulfill.

Effective leaders are not at the mercy of external forces that lie beyond their control. They are guided by an internal compass, taking consistent action to live purposefully. They create their own success as a result of rededicating themselves to their vision on a daily basis.

Each moment, you have the power of choice. Choose to do something that aligns you with your vision, rather than things that keep you entrenched in old habits or beliefs. Stay hungry! Guard against complacency. You have the power to accomplish a great purpose with your life—if you choose to do so. **Why do what most people can or will, when you can do what most people can't or won't?**

Application

Place your vision statement where you and the people in your organization can look at it each day. Ascertain that it aligns with your core values and sense of purpose. Write it with descriptive adjectives that stimulate

Tom Massey

passion and enthusiasm. Establish long- and short-term goals that are designed to move you toward your vision. Conduct regular meetings to evaluate progress and how those goals are staying aligned with your purpose. Visualize success and encourage others to do likewise.

As a leader of power and intelligence, and the master of your own thoughts, you hold the key to triumph in every situation. Keep aligned with your vision and move toward it each day!

Affirmation

I am powerfully aligned with my vision as I lead with a sense of clarity and purpose.

Know When

22

...To put dead issues to rest!

*C*huck had an old hunting dog that he had grown quite fond of over the past fifteen years. One day the dog became really sick. He was lifeless when Chuck found him lying behind the house that morning. Chuck loaded the dog up in his pickup and headed to the local veterinary clinic. When he arrived, the vet's assistant instructed him to carry his dog to the examining room and lay it down on the table. When the vet came in, he checked the dog's vital signs and told Chuck, "Sir, I'm sorry to have to tell you, but your dog is dead."

"Why, that's ridiculous!" Chuck demanded, "I want another opinion!" A Labrador retriever then entered the room and sniffed the dog from one end to the other. The retriever looked up at Chuck and nodded, "Yep, this dog is dead."

Chuck refused to believe it. "I want another opinion," he cried. Next, a cat came into the room, jumped up on the table and carefully inched her way up one side of the dog and down the other. She looked up and nodded in concurrence with the vet and the Labrador retriever, "This dog is dead."

Chuck still refused to believe it. He picked up his dog and stomped out, muttering something about another opinion. The office assistant handed him the bill on his way out the door. When Chuck got to his truck he looked at the bill and shrieked, "Three hundred dollars?!" He marched back in and confronted the veterinarian. "What is the meaning of this? Three hundred dollars just to tell me my dog is dead?"

The vet looked at Chuck, shook his head apologetically and replied, "Sir, your bill was only going to be fifty dollars, but I had to charge you for the Lab report and the cat scan."

Tom Massey

Like the fellow in this story, many of us carry around old dogs that need to be put to rest. Those old dogs may be regrets from failed plans, strategies, or partnerships that no longer serve us. For whatever reason, we hold on to them, carrying them around like a smelly old carcass, deceiving ourselves into thinking they are still useful.

As a leader, there will be times when you'll have to choose between cutting your losses and moving on, or continuing to carry a dead dog. **Effective leaders make choices based on what is best for the present and the future.**

Application

Are there some old dogs that you need to put to rest? Perhaps you've made some past decisions that didn't pan out. Instead of looking back with regret or continuing on because you don't want to admit defeat, clean the slate and launch out on a fresh start. Not every decision you make or plan you devise will be a beaming success. And not every person you hire will be a stellar employee. Learn from your actions, make adjustments, and move forward.

This message is not about knee-jerk reactions or impulsiveness. It is not about giving up when the going gets tough. Instead, it is about making deliberate, calculated decisions to take the best course of action, without guilt or a sense of failure. At times the most prudent thing you can do is to put that old dog to rest.

Affirmation

I have the power to create success by making decisions that best affect the present and the future.

Leave Your Comfort Zone

23

Jump . . . and the courage will follow!

Sharon went on a hike in the mountains of Wyoming with a woman who was a local trail guide. The scenery was breathtaking as they wound their way through vista after vista on a looping trail that the woman had charted out for them. They were about six hours into their hike when they came to a place where the trail appeared to dead-end overlooking a river that gently flowed about 30 feet below them.

Sharon became inquisitive of her companion, who seemed undaunted by their situation. The woman told her that the trail continued on the other side of the river. They could simply make the leap into the river below and swim across. Sharon was a good swimmer, but she was a bit squeamish at the thought of jumping into a river some 30 feet below. She expressed her fears openly. Her guide explained that they were only about two hours from the trailhead if they continued forward, but if they turned around it would take over six hours to return the way they came. By that time it would be getting cold and dark. She told Sharon that she understood her fearfulness, but assured her that the best way to go was forward. "All you have to do is jump," she said, "the courage will follow."

Sometimes life requires a leap of faith. You may experience fear and perhaps entertain the thought of retreating to avoid having to make the leap. But in many situations, the best direction to go is forward. Don't allow fear or timidity to stand in the way of your reaching your highest potential.

Effective leaders are risk-takers, willing to step out of their own comfort zones to forge new paths. They realize that the exploration of new frontiers yields magnificent discoveries of knowledge and resources. A leap of faith into the unknown unlocks doors not yet imagined. **A life that has been stretched rarely returns to its original dimensions.**

Application

When was the last time you took a leap of faith? How long has it been since you were stretched out of your comfort zone? There are many ways you can do this in a controlled environment that offers safety and support. One of the best ways is to participate in an outdoor challenge course. Ropes courses or Outward Bound excursions are excellent for assisting you in stretching beyond your personal fears. These are also great team-building activities that will empower your organization toward outstanding performances. By taking the initiative to walk through your own fears, you'll give others permission to do the same.

Affirmation

I fearlessly step out of my comfort zone to explore and experience life to the fullest.

Let Go of the Outcome

24

... And enjoy the process!

*O*prah Winfrey poured ten years of her life into the making of the movie *Beloved*. She wanted to create something so powerful that it would cause people to truly feel what it meant to overcome slavery. This wasn't just a story about a period in history. This was about real people, her ancestors, who overcame tremendous adversity to regain their sense of humanity and reconstruct their lives in ordinary and extraordinary ways.

Although Oprah considered this to be one of her life's greatest accomplishments, it made only $23 million at the box office, a failure by Hollywood standards. She was disheartened and depressed for months, until she came to the realization that her problem was not the movie, but her attachment to the outcome. Hollywood's standards were not her own. She had followed her vision and made a movie she thought the world deserved to see. For that, she felt fulfilled and grateful. She said, "The experience opened me up to know that if my ancestors could survive with so little, then I, who have been given so much, can surely be triumphant. No box-office returns can ever diminish that."

You may occasionally make decisions or direct projects that are rejected or deemed a failure by the world's standards. That does not make you a failure or define who you are. Every experience is an opportunity to learn and grow.

The road to success may be filled with detours, curves, uphill climbs, or downhill slides, but your experience will be defined by how you choose to respond. **Effective leaders let go of their attachment to the outcome and find purpose in the process.**

Application

Do you have the courage to pursue your dream, regardless of what others think? It's a good idea to listen to feedback from others, but do not judge your success by their opinions. And don't give your power away to failure. It may be an indication that you need to make some adjustments in what you are doing, but failure doesn't define who you are. Commit to do your best in the present moment, without being sabotaged by regrets of the past or fear of how others may judge you. Live from the inside out.

Affirmation

I release my attachment to outcome and enjoy the process, as I do my best each day to learn from life's experiences.

Manage by Mingling 25

Get out of your office!

I once knew a manager who rarely mingled with the "hired help"—his term for employees. If he wanted something from his constituents, he would summon them to his office. And those meetings were always akin to being taken to the woodshed, because he only called people to his office to deliver criticism. He said he came from the old school that believes people should be left alone when they're doing a good job, and given a talking-to when they're not. I call that the "treat people like mushrooms" style of management—feed 'em manure and keep 'em in the dark.

I learned a lot about leadership from that man. Unfortunately, most of it was what *not* to do. His management style may have been good for mushrooms, but it wasn't very effective with people.

Management by mingling is a much more communicative style of leadership that enables managers to become actively engaged in the day-to-day activities of the business. This is a high-profile approach that works well for giving continuous feedback and encouragement. It permits all employees to have direct access to the boss and frequently generates high levels of spontaneous, creative synergy from the exchange of ideas.

Effective leaders know the value and impact of management by mingling. It gives them a chance to feel the pulse beat while infusing an energetic boost into the lifeblood of the organization. By remaining accessible, these leaders become coaches, mentors, cheerleaders, and catalysts for outstanding performances and commitment to excellence. Expand your awareness and skills in this area to **increase meaningful contact with and impact on the people in your organization.**

Application

Do you use management by mingling within your organization? First, be aware that this approach must be carried out authentically. Don't force it or treat it like a game of charades. People will quickly see through it if you are "doing this just to be doing it." Be yourself. That way you'll be much more effective moving throughout the organization looking for opportunities to make positive comments or receive input and feedback. It is important to be honest and genuine. Don't patronize people or offer superficial flattery.

Mingling will allow you to see everything going on, and it will allow you to listen directly to the employees. It is especially effective if you lead an organization with many management layers or if you are faced with the challenge of extending this concept with staffs that are geographically dispersed. You can extend your impact by learning how to leverage new tools and groupware technologies that will allow you to "manage by mingling" online. Be creative, set up web-based chat rooms or media for interactive dialogues with your employees through your computer network.

Affirmation

I increase my effectiveness as a leader by regularly practicing management by mingling.

Manage Conflict Creatively

26

Stay cool and think "Win–Win"!

*O*ne evening Linda Lantieri, the founder and director of the New York City-based Resolving Conflict Creatively Program, was walking down a deserted, perilous-looking block lined with vacant, boarded-up buildings. Out of nowhere, three teenage boys surrounded her and pulled out a knife as they pressed closely around her.

"Give me your purse! Now!" the boy with the knife demanded.

Though terrified, Linda had the presence of mind to take some deep breaths and reply coolly, "I'm feeling a little uncomfortable. You know, guys, you're a little into my space. I'm wondering if you could step back a little."

She kept her gaze on the sidewalk—and to her amazement, she saw three pairs of sneakers take a few steps back. "Thank you," she said, "Now, I want to hear what you just said to me, but to tell you the truth, I'm a little nervous about that knife. I'm wondering if you could put it away."

After what seemed an eternity of silence and indecision, the boy slipped the knife back into his pocket. Linda quickly reached into her purse and pulled out a twenty-dollar bill, catching the eye of the boy with the knife. "Whom should I give this to?" she asked.

"Me," he said. She glanced at the other two and asked if they agreed. One of them nodded. "Great," she said, handing the boy the twenty-dollar bill. "Now here's what's going to happen. I'm going to stay right here while you walk away."

With puzzled looks on their faces, the boys slowly began to walk away. Then they glanced over their shoulders at Linda and actually began to *run from her.*

Hopefully, you will never have to negotiate your way out of a precarious situation like the one just described. But negotiations, mostly on an informal basis, take place all the time in business. **Effective leaders espouse win–win solutions through self-awareness, self-confidence, self-control, and empathy.**

Application

Negotiation skills obviously matter a great deal for effectiveness in leadership. Through practicing solid conflict-resolution techniques, you will be better able to influence others to their benefit, as well as your own. Here are some practical tips for cooling down any tense situation:

1. First, take a deep breath and calm down.
2. Tune into your feelings and express them in a nonthreatening way.
3. Express a willingness to work things out by talking over the issue rather than escalating it with more aggression.
4. State your own point of view in a nonargumentative tone, without directing blame or putting the other person on the defensive.
5. Attempt to find equitable resolutions to the dispute that both sides will embrace as win–win.

Affirmation

I am effective at resolving conflict by staying cool and going for win–win solutions.

New Directions

27

Trickle-up leadership!

*I*n his new book, *Leading Up: How to Lead Your Boss So You Both Win,*
Wharton management professor Michael Useem cites General
Electric, under the leadership of CEO Jack Welch, as making massive
strides in embracing the concept of "trickle-up" leadership. At GE everyone is expected to challenge his or her leaders, even if it means challenging Welch himself.

Up until two years ago, GE required all senior management members
to mentor the next generation of the company's top talent. At that time,
Welch observed, "E-business knowledge is generally inversely propor-
tional to both age and height in the organization." To counterbalance this
phenomenon, the company launched a "reverse mentoring" program, in
which six hundred executives worldwide were asked to reach down into
the ranks and pick younger people to mentor them on the intricacies of
the Internet and Web development. Welch set the example by choosing
his own Net coach, Pam Wickham, who ran GE's main Web site.

The mentoring sessions did more than give executives Web site and
e-business orientations. It opened the lines of communication for leadership to flow both upward and downward much more easily within the
organization. The mid-level managers felt more comfortable in feeding
ideas to their bosses and pressing change at the top. And top-level managers experienced a greater sense of ease in eliciting insights from below.
The entire organization benefited from the process.

Effective leaders don't have confidence in yes-men and yes-women, the
kind that are afraid to speak up when "the emperor has no clothes." These
leaders not only encourage it, they expect to be challenged when orders
are flawed. They never end a meeting without asking constituents to state

what they think. **By challenging others to challenge them, effective leaders create a culture where everyone is inspired to lead up.**

Application

Do you encourage people to lead up? Or are they too intimidated or reluctant to speak what's on their mind? If people are afraid to help you lead, you are setting yourself and the organization up for failure. Workers on the front lines of the business are closer to markets and closer to how products are used. Often, they can see what you are missing.

This issue is *not* about arguing up rather than leading up. I do not mean that people should disagree with you every time a directive is given. And it is certainly not in their or your best interest to publicly argue each point. Sometimes discretion is the better part of valor, and political savvy is about knowing when to ask certain questions or make specific points.

It is important for a leader to coach people on how to speak in such a way that they can be heard. Some issues are best discussed behind closed doors, and a collaborative style is always preferable to a confrontational style.

Affirmation

I reinforce a culture where leadership flows in all directions, and I expect to be challenged when people within the organization see a better way.

Never
Underestimate

28

...The power of a small group—they can change the world!

*A*s a young man, I felt a calling to a ministry of evangelism. I had visions of conducting crusades, filling stadiums with people, and becoming the world's next Billy Graham. One morning, I passionately shared my dream with a man who had been my teacher and spiritual counselor for a number of years.

He listened quietly to my animated vision of how multitudes of people would hear my sermons and experience transformational life changes. When I finished, he gazed at me intently and said with a slight grin, "If you sling enough s___ against the wall, I suppose some of it will stick."

I was astonished and puzzled by these words uttered by the most spiritual person I knew. I quickly asked him to explain. He said, "I have no doubt that you have the charisma and enthusiasm to reach tens, perhaps hundreds, of thousands of people. But you don't really know what lasting impact you will have on their lives.

"Instead," he said, "why not pour your life into ten other people, and have each one of them pour their life into ten others, and each one of those pour their life into ten others, and so on.

"You get the picture?" he asked. "Then, you have an exponential growth in numbers, filled with lasting quality. That's what I call the 'kingdom' principle," he explained. "I didn't invent it, Jesus did, and look at the impact He had on the world."

I have never forgotten my friend's advice. Since that time, I have seen this principle work time and again within various organizations. Effective leaders understand the power of mentoring and working with small groups. As anthropologist Margaret Mead once said, **"Never doubt that** a small group of thoughtful and committed citizens can change the world; indeed, it's the only thing that ever has."

Application

How are you impacting your organization? Are you mentoring and nurturing small groups to grow in leadership abilities? Try becoming a R.E.A.L. leader, which means:

Responsive
Empathetic
Affirming
Listener

Respond to situations and people with decisive, deliberate action. Empathize with the needs of others by showing sensitivity and understanding for their perspective. Affirm people by acknowledging their contribution and value to the organization. Listen attentively to concerns, desires, and feedback of others, with enthusiasm and open-mindedness.

Affirmation

I am a R.E.A.L. leader who appreciates and utilizes the power of small groups.

Online 29

Are you connected?

*F*or those of us who were raised in the "Father Knows Best" era, life has changed drastically. It appears that the world is no longer stable or predictable. The Industrial Age has given way to the Information/Technology Age and dot-com companies. Digital energy has affected every business strategy, from launching products and serving customers to organizing creativity and productivity.

Leaders are continually called upon to challenge conventional wisdom within their industries and in their companies. To succeed, they must be open to new ideas, new practices, and new opportunities, willing to reinvent, reenergize, and redirect all matters of business at a moment's notice. In the I/T Age, the large, sturdy, traditional businesses are being radically pushed aside by nimble, agile, Web-based operations.

To be sure, astonishing innovations and dramatic changes are being unleashed throughout the world. Knowledge has skyrocketed, computers have become super, genetics are being altered, and even geopolitics have been reshaped—all because of rapidly changing technology. And this is just the beginning!

Effective leaders are able to embrace change and innovation, while at the same time grasping the value of the individual and the scope of opportunity that exists for people. Never before in the history of business has the individual mattered more or the opportunities been so great. People are not just anonymous cogs in the gigantic technological machine. The world still depends on the unit of one—that inspired leader, that talented performer, that creative inventor, that consumer in the marketplace. **Regardless of the age or advancement of technology, business will always be fueled by People Power!**

Tom Massey

Application

How does your leadership scorecard look for the new millennium? Are you creating an environment that is fertile for the exchange of ideas? Free for trying new things? Fast enough to keep up with the speed-of-light changes that are taking place?

Pay attention to people. Create a learning organization. Management guru Tom Peters coined the term SAV, which stands for "Screw Around Vigorously." He says that the most important kind of speed today is the speed of learning. There's no substitute for getting smarter faster, and the way to do that is to "screw around vigorously."

Can you think of a time when work was so compelling and engaging? The future is not just about dot-coms. Nor is it about rising stock markets or venture capitalists. The future of business is about the never-ceasing opportunities for passionate, fully engaged, motivated individuals.

Affirmation

I stay online with people to freely exchange information and ideas to create better ways of doing business.

Ordinary People   30

...Perform extraordinary acts!

*M*ost historians believe that the modern civil rights movement in the United States began on December 1, 1955, in Montgomery, Alabama, when an unknown seamstress named Rosa Parks refused to give up her bus seat to a white passenger. This woman was arrested and fined for violating a city ordinance, but her lonely act of defiance began a movement that ended legal segregation in America, and made her an inspiration to freedom-loving people everywhere. Dr. Martin Luther King later recalled, "Rosa Parks sat anchored to that seat by the accumulated indignities of days gone by, and the countless aspirations of generations yet unborn."

Interestingly, when we look across the history of the civil rights movement, we acknowledge people like Abraham Lincoln, who pushed the Congress of that era to enact constitutional amendments to protect personal freedom. We celebrate visionaries such as William Lloyd Garrison and Frederick Douglass. We applaud the bravery of Dwight Eisenhower for sending the troops to Little Rock, and the commitment of John and Robert Kennedy to embrace civil rights for all people.

Ultimately, we must know that it is the people who have no position or money, and have only the power of their courage and character, who forge new paths for public leaders to follow. Often these individuals are unaware of the magnitude of their own heroics. Rosa Parks admitted, "I didn't get on the bus to get arrested. I got on that bus to go home."

Effective leaders keep their eyes and ears open for uncommon situations championed by common people. They remain attuned to the winds of change that are echoed by these voices crying out, beckoning the masses to listen and take action. **Behind every great leader stand ordinary people with the courage to perform extraordinary acts!**

Application

Who are the Rosa Parkses in your organization? Are you listening to the unsung heroes and visionaries who point the way to greatness? Sometimes the extraordinary happens in the most ordinary moments. But then again, there are no ordinary moments. We are constantly presented with opportunities to improve, to expand, to grow, to learn, or to act.

When was the last time you were truly inspired? Was it during an emotionally moving speech or public celebration? Those are easy. The real test of your character as an effective leader is whether you become inspired in those moments when no one is watching. Those moments when you see a wrong and privately try to correct it, or acknowledge others who are willing to anonymously stand up and make a difference.

If you want to impact the world, first change your thinking. Think of yourself as a leader who creates extraordinary opportunities for ordinary people.

Affirmation

I look and listen for the ordinary people with the courage to perform extraordinary acts.

Perception Shapes Reality

31

The story heard is the story told!

A nationally known singer and songwriter who is reputedly terrified of performing in front of a live audience was once asked what she experiences before going on stage. She responded, "I get butterflies in my stomach. My palms begin to sweat. My heart begins to pound. And I feel like I'm going to have a nervous breakdown."

Another prominent entertainer, who thrives on performing for live audiences, was asked the same question about his experiences before taking the stage. He replied, "I get butterflies in my stomach. My palms begin to sweat. My heart begins to pound. And then I know I'm ready!"

Each of these performers experiences the same physiological responses going into similar situations, but each has a different perception of reality, based on their own emotional programming. Consequently, each has an internal dialogue about the experience. The first is telling herself a story about fear and anxiety, while the other tells himself that the increased emotional energy is serving to exhilarate his performance.

Our perceptions shape our reality. We each have a choice. We can let circumstances rule our lives, or we can respond by moving through those circumstances, regardless of how unpleasant they appear, choosing to live with purpose.

Effective leaders possess a high degree of emotional and mental determination. They keep telling themselves a positive story as they move undauntedly toward their goals.

Many great leaders who have been considered successful in their field have faced major setbacks:

• Abraham Lincoln lost eight elections and failed twice in business.

- Walt Disney, who was dyslexic as a child, lost his first cartoon production company to bankruptcy.
- Dr. Seuss's first book was rejected by twenty-seven publishers.
- John Grisham's first book was rejected by sixteen agents and twelve publishers.
- Michael Jordan was cut from his high school's varsity football team as a sophomore.

These are just a few examples of determined people who have overcome perceived failures and experienced great success. They all kept telling themselves the story: **"I think I can! I think I can!"**

Application

What story do you tell yourself when faced with fear or adversity? Do you use that adrenaline-driven energy to motivate yourself to perform at higher levels, or do you allow it to reduce you to a nervous wreck? You have the power to choose your response in any situation. Become aware that faulty perceptions, based on emotional programming from your past, may at times cause defeating beliefs. Start changing those beliefs by using positive self-talk. Begin to tell yourself a different story. And encourage others to do the same.

Affirmation

I am aware that perception shapes my reality and use positive self-talk to move boldly through fear.

Play To Win

32

...Instead of playing not to lose!

*M*y son had above-average athletic talent and played baseball competitively as a youth. I remember one particular coach who was a nice guy most of the time, but suffered from Jekyll-and-Hyde syndrome in the clutch. When his team was winning, he was the most positive person around. But when the heat was on and his team was down, he fell apart emotionally and became overly critical, which caused the kids to tighten up and play not to lose. After one of their losses, I asked my son what he thought about when he went to bat when his team was behind. He said, "I think about what will happen if I strike out."

That same fear runs rampant throughout many organizations today, where employees are thinking about what will happen if they strike out, rather than relishing the thought of hitting a homerun. When people are playing not to lose, they become tense. They refuse to take risks because the consequences of any failed action begin to produce more fear than the prospect of success. This can lead to a vicious cycle of fear–loss–fear–loss–fear–loss.

Effective leaders understand how to turn moments of fear and uncertainty into opportunities for ordinary people to achieve extraordinary results. The late Hall-of-Fame coaching legend, John Wooden, once told his UCLA basketball team, "Men, the team that makes the most mistakes tonight will win the game!" He encouraged his players to take risks and make more mistakes because he knew that you miss 100 percent of the shots you never take. Wooden was one of the most successful coaches in the history of college basketball because he understood how to create an environment where people play to win.

Focus on winning, rather than losing, and your team will play with confidence and lights-out abandon—all the stops pulled out and no holds barred. **When the going gets tough, the tough play to win!**

Application

How do you react when the going gets tough and your team falls behind? Does the fear of losing immobilize you? Or are you inspired to perform at higher levels? Here are a few suggestions for playing to win:

1. Work up a great game plan by identifying the key results you want to achieve.
2. Maximize your strengths and minimize your weaknesses by focusing on what you do well.
3. Simplify by concentrating on the most important issues, one at a time.
4. Have fun and *think positive*! Your optimism is contagious.

The game of life is your shot at the championship. Stay loose and play with passion. You may be surprised at how great the results will be when you stop worrying about losing.

Affirmation

I play to win and savor each moment as an opportunity to perform in extraordinary ways.

Quality Training 33

Attitudes follow behaviors!

The U.S. Department of Labor recently published a report identifying the major strengths that American workers fundamentally lack. These include skills in problem solving, developing technical innovations, interpersonal communication, working with a team, and getting along with their boss. Another study by the American Society for Training and Development revealed that workers consistently see their managers and supervisors as confused about performance expectations, slow to respond to serious problems, and unable to articulate a clear vision for their groups. The simple truth is: New skills and new attitudes are currently needed at every organizational level.

One solution to this dilemma is quality training. And the benchmark training methodology is behavior modeling. This experience-based technique is highly effective in teaching people new interpersonal or technical skills, as well as the knowledge of why, when, and how to use the skills. When they return to the job, people experience heightened self-esteem and positive attitudes about their work because new skills bring increased recognition and satisfaction for a job well done.

The principles behind behavior modeling may best be described by the words of ancient Chinese philosopher Confucius, who wrote, "I hear and I forget. I see and I remember. I do and I understand." Following these principles, Hippocrates learned the art of healing, Churchill learned to orate, and Mozart learned to play the piano.

Effective leaders understand that behavior modeling can be a catalyst for wide-range corporate growth. This type of training facilitates behavioral change at every level of the organization by helping people improve how they work, how they feel about their work, and how they perceive leadership. **Transformation begins not in the boardroom, but in the classroom.**

Application

Behavior modeling offers a blueprint for accelerated learning. Students first observe the clear demonstration of a skill, then emulate it to build competence and self-confidence. They are given the opportunity to practice new skills and to plan their own practical application, in a safe environment with constructive, performance-enhancing feedback. A typical behavior-modeling training program would include the following steps:

1. Describe the performance areas of a skill and why they are important.
2. Solicit feedback from participants on how the training might be enhanced or customized to more suitably meet their needs and requirements.
3. Demonstrate the skill components in a manner that is effective for a wide range of learning styles, including audio, visual, and kinesthetic.
4. Set up training opportunities for participants to practice the skill repeatedly with constructive feedback.
5. Allow participants to reflect on specific practical applications of the skill.
6. Express confidence and support.
7. Provide a summary of the items covered and arrange a follow-up date for ongoing feedback and performance evaluation.

Affirmation

I am creating a high-performance organization through quality training.

Quit Demotivating 34

. . . And be aware of unhealthy competition!

*A*s I travel across the country meeting with groups of workers, one of the standard questions I pose is, "What is the biggest demotivator you encounter within your organization?" The topic that surfaces over and over is the employee-of-the-month award. How can this be? This award is supposed to motivate people. I doubt if anyone ever thought, "Let's alienate a bunch of people in the organization by picking an employee of the month."

What might have originally been intended to be beneficial may ultimately be counterproductive. The complaint I hear most about the employee-of-the-month award is that the recognition is given to "butt-kissers" and "brown-nosers." Workers claim that the real employees of the month are those unsung heroes faithfully working behind the scenes with little regard for recognition and awards. I can't argue with that.

I'm not saying that employee awards are bad. What I am saying is that awards and individual bonuses should be administered in a sensitive manner, so as not to demotivate people or promote unhealthy competition. What is the benefit of making one individual happy at the risk of alienating a hundred? There has to be a better way to recognize people.

Effective leaders are good-finders. They don't wait for the annual performance review or monthly awards ceremony to applaud great effort. When they catch people doing a good job, they acknowledge them immediately as the "employee of the moment." Effective leaders don't pit employees against one another in a vicious race to see who gets the one performance bonus to be doled out. Instead, they place an emphasis on team contribution and involvement to promote a collaborative work environment where everyone shares the wealth. **There is no "I" in "team"!**

Application

Are you a good-finder? Do you acknowledge outstanding performance when it happens? If you currently present an employee-of-the-month award, solicit candid feedback about the feelings it generates within the organization. Is it a source of motivation or demotivation? If it is a demo-tivator, solicit ideas from your team about how you can administer this award more effectively or eliminate it.

Are you creating healthy competition within the work environment by promoting team unity? Rather than doling out year-end bonuses based solely on individual performance, think about how you can create a "share the wealth" mentality through group rewards.

Affirmation

I motivate people by sensitively acknowledging individual performance and promote healthy competition by applauding team effort.

Respond Instead of Reacting 35

Pull your own strings!

*T*he scene took place over forty years ago, when I was in first grade. A playground bully was picking on one of my friends. The kid, who was a couple of years older and about a foot taller, had my friend in a head lock and seemed about to choke him to death. During the ruckus, an ink pen fell out of the bully's shirt pocket. I ran over, picked it up, and threw it on top of the school building to distract him.

This distracted him, all right. He yelled and squealed as if someone had stabbed him with a knife. He lamented that the ink pen belonged to his father and now he was in big, big trouble.

The kid ran into the building and told my teacher what I'd done, playing the role of the innocent victim. My teacher, who could have passed for a Marine Corps drill instructor, came charging out, grabbed me by the seat of the pants and began to whip me furiously. (In those days it was not only legal for teachers to whip children, some felt it was their civic duty to dole out a daily beating.) She refused to hear any explanation that I had to give about the matter.

The school janitor was summoned to bring a ladder and retrieve the ink pen from the top of the building. While he was performing this task, the bell rang, signaling that recess was over and it was time to go back into class. As usual, we lined up in single file and waited for the teacher to give us the cue to go inside. She was still stomping around directing the janitor on the pen-retrieval mission. Every minute or so she would come over, angrily jerk me out of line, and apply a few more well-placed swats to the bottom. The spanking didn't really hurt that much, but the whole scene became rather humiliating and confusing, especially for a small child who had performed a desperate act to save a friend's neck.

This was a defining moment in my life. It left an emotional mark that affected the way I viewed authority figures for the next thirty years. Often, without understanding why, I reacted to leaders with cynicism and mistrust. Finally, I became aware of these patterns of behavior and the critical choices I was making because of that one long-ago incident. Through awareness came the power to change! Now, instead of reacting to people or situations in knee-jerk fashion, based on old data, I choose to respond in ways that are more constructive and appropriate for current situations.

Effective leaders live in the moment, but acknowledge the influence of the past. They are aware of their own internal triggers or hot buttons, and how others may push them. Effective leadership requires a high degree of emotional intelligence, which begins with self-awareness. **Know yourself!**

Application

What were your defining moments? Are there certain issues or scenarios that keep repeating in your life? The names have changed, but the same characters keep showing up again and again. Take some time this week for personal reflection and self-inventory. Pay attention to how past experiences have affected your life choices and relationships. You can rewrite the script, but first you must become aware.

Try this little exercise in awareness and self-control: The next time you have an itch, don't immediately scratch it. Instead, focus on the itch, think about its origin, and allow yourself to feel it without doing anything about it. Often, it will go away by itself if you direct your attention toward it long enough.

Learn to apply this discipline to emotional itches, as well. The next time you have an urge to react to a person or situation, stop and focus on what is happening. Think about what you really feel, then mentally trace the origin of that feeling. You may find that the emotion, like the itch, goes away when you focus your attention toward it. If not, you have at least allowed yourself time to respond rather than react.

Affirmation

A *wareness of defining moments and emotional imprints empowers me to respond to current situations rather than reacting.*

Risks

What is greatness worth?

B ob Manley, a copyeditor for a Cleveland newspaper, was a man some people might have called crazy. Dreaming of retracing the immigration route of his ancestors, he set his sights on sailing from Falmouth, Massachusetts, to Falmouth, England.

For less than a few hundred dollars, Bob purchased a thirty-year-old sailboat that measured only thirteen-and-a-half feet. He refurbished the boat and practiced sailing on Lake Erie for several months. To avoid hearing the discouraging words of nay-sayers, he shared his plans only with his wife.

On the day of embarkation, Bob kissed his wife and set sail on the 3200-mile voyage, tying himself to his boat in case he encountered rough seas that threatened to toss him overboard. This turned out to be a wise precaution, because he was thrown from the sailboat several times by storm-tossed waves. To make matters worse, he had to remain awake at night to avoid entering the shipping lanes. With his sleep limited to daytime naps, Bob became delirious and exhausted. Yet he sailed onward.

Seventy-eight days later, he sailed into the harbor at Falmouth, England, to a reception of over twenty thousand people who had heard about his remarkable feat. Because of his achievement, one U.S. congressman submitted a bill to place Bob's boat, "Tinker Bell," next to Charles Lindbergh's "Spirit of Saint Louis" in the Smithsonian Institute. When asked why he would attempt such an incredible challenge, Bob Manley answered, "There comes a time when one must decide either to risk everything to fulfill one's dream, or sit for the rest of one's life in the backyard."

Effective leaders are risk-takers—pacesetters willing to act upon their vision and goals. They are undaunted by the pessimistic "we've never done

Tom Massey

it that way before" crowd. They set their course and weather each storm in pursuit of a heroic destiny. **Life is a daring adventure or nothing at all . . . Take a risk!**

Application

Are you pursuing greatness as a leader? Have you pushed yourself or your organization to limits that will create a clearer understanding of what you can do and what you can become? What old paradigms are you still operating under that need to be changed or expanded?

You have the power to do things you never dreamed possible. This power becomes available to you as soon as you are willing to change your beliefs and take action. If you did all the things you're capable of doing, you would literally amaze yourself.

You know what you are today, but not what you may become tomorrow. Look at life as you want it to be, and then make things happen. Bold intentions lead to courageous actions, which result in astounding outcomes. You never know what you can do until you try.

Affirmation

I am a risk-taker who fearlessly takes action to achieve outstanding results.

Skip the Comparison

37

Individuality is a gift!

*I*n *The Tassajara Bread Book*, Zen teacher Edward Espe Brown described a great truth that he learned from his kitchen practice. When Edward first started cooking, he couldn't get biscuits to come out the way they were supposed to. He would follow a recipe and try variations, but nothing worked. His biscuits just didn't measure up to the Bisquick and Pillsbury biscuits he had made while growing up.

It didn't seem fair. Those biscuits of his youth were so easy to make. For the Bisquick, all you had to do was add milk to the mix and blob the dough in spoonfuls onto the pan—they didn't even need to be rolled out. The biscuits from Pillsbury came in a cardboard can. You just popped them open, put the premade biscuits on a pan, and baked them. They came out right every time. Now that's what biscuits were supposed to be like—Bisquick and Pillsbury.

Edward grew frustrated because, to his way of thinking, his biscuits never turned out right, even though the people who ate them would extol their virtues, eating one after another. In his mind, these perfectly good biscuits just weren't right, until one day Edward had an awakening, a real "ah-hah" experience, about his biscuits.

"Not right, compared to what?" he asked himself. All this time he had been trying to make canned biscuits. Then came the revelation of tasting his biscuits without comparing them to some preconceived standard. They were wheaty, flaky, buttery, light, and earthy. They were exquisitely alive—in fact, they were much more satisfying than any memory of canned biscuits.

A moment of liberation comes when you realize that your life is fine just as it is. Only the insidious comparison to a neatly scripted, beautifully

Tom Massey

packaged product made it seem insignificant or insufficient. You may have spent years striving to "look perfect" like the Bisquick leader, always calm, directed, energetic, and collected. Trying to produce a biscuit—a life—with no dirty bowls, no messy feelings or hindrances, can be a frustrating experience. **Effective leaders possess the wisdom to appreciate and celebrate individuality.**

Application

Are you a Bisquick leader, always trying to fit yourself and others into a neatly packaged plan? Or are you willing to allow people to cook their own biscuits from scratch? Standards are fine. We need them to ensure continuity and quality of performance. But workers also need a sense of independence without constantly being compared to or expected to perform exactly like others. If you try to hold someone accountable for work, but give her little say in how to go about it, you will eventually lower morale and job performance.

Micromanagement leads to frustration when people see ways to do their work better, but are held back by rigid standards. This diminishes levels of responsibility, flexibility, and innovation. The emotional message to workers is: The company lacks respect for their judgment and innate abilities. Give yourself and others permission to be unique.

Affirmation

I celebrate individuality and encourage innovation in others and myself.

Speak

38

...In such a way that you can be heard!

*H*arvard social psychologist Ellen Langer once conducted an experiment to prove a theory of human behavior that states: When we ask someone to do something, we will be more successful if we provide a reason. One of the tests she used was to ask a group of people waiting in line to use a library copying machine the following question: "Excuse me, I have five pages. May I use the copy machine?" Of the respondents she asked, sixty percent agreed to allow her to cut in front of them.

Langer conducted another test where she asked a group the question: "Excuse me, I have five pages. May I use the copy machine *because* I'm in a rush?" The effectiveness of this request-with-a-reason increased drastically over the first. Ninety-four percent of those she asked allowed her to skip ahead of them in line.

At first glance, it appeared that the critical difference between the two requests was solely because of the additional information provided by the words, "because I'm in a rush." However, Langer repeated the experiment a third time, restating the question this way: "Excuse me, I have five pages. May I use the copy machine *because* I have to make some copies?" Once again the effectiveness of the question was nearly total. Ninety-three percent of those she asked let her move ahead of them in the copy line, their compliance triggered simply by using the word "because" and a restatement of the obvious.

Human behavior doesn't always work in such a mechanical way, but it is astonishing how often it does. When people are given a simple "because," they'll comply with almost any request. Effective leaders understand the art of persuasiveness. Speak in such a way that people hear you. **When you ask someone to do something, always give a "because."**

Application

How persuasive are you as a leader? Do you speak in such a way as to be heard? Do people readily comply with your requests? When you give others the benefit of knowing the reasoning behind your requests, they feel respected and validated. They will respond with reciprocity and compliance. Remember the old adage: "You'll draw more flies with honey."

This is not about psychologically manipulating others to do what you ask. I simply encourage you to be considerate and use this common-sense approach to persuasiveness—explain why when you ask people to do something. When you speak in such a way that you can be heard, your influence as a leader will soar.

Affirmation

I speak in such a way that I can be heard, by being considerate of others and always offering a reason for making requests.

Take Charge 39

Become a catalyst for transformation!

*I*t was a snowy, desperate day at the Denver International Airport. Flight after flight had been canceled, and lines at the airlines' service desks were snaking out of sight. Tension and tempers had been building by the hour, with customers sniping at the airline representatives—and at one another.

As I stood in line, feeling the pulse beat of the mob beginning to rise to frantic levels, I decided to try to change the mood—at least of those near me. So I announced, "I'm going to get some coffee, anyone else want something to drink?"

I took down orders that echoed from a growing chorus of frustrated passengers, hustled off to the nearest coffee shop, and returned with a tray filled with drinks. That one act was enough to trigger a wave of good feelings and lightheartedness among the group.

For that short moment, I emerged as the unofficial leader of this loosely knit group of stranded travelers. Their attitude improved and their mood softened. The airline representatives even began to respond differently, without an air of defensiveness. I experienced firsthand the fluid role of a leader as a catalyst for transformation.

Effective leaders transform people through the sheer power of their own enthusiasm. They don't order or direct; they inspire. You may be called upon to come forward to take a leadership role for a time, then fade back into the group. Such a move requires self-confidence and initiative. Articulate a plan that excites people's imaginations and inspires them to change their thinking. Be bold. Be creative. **It takes more than authority to motivate and lead.**

Tom Massey

Application

To become a catalyst for transformation, you must first recognize the need for change and be willing to take some bold steps to remove the barriers. Don't be afraid to challenge the status quo and acknowledge the need to do things differently. Start thinking "outside the box." As you champion the change, enlist others in your pursuit and lead by example. Adopt the following leadership characteristics:

1. Be enthusiastic, positive, and outgoing.
2. Be emotionally expressive.
3. Be cooperative and democratic.
4. Be sociable and friendly (including smiling more).
5. Be appreciative and trustful.

Affirmation

I am a catalyst for transformation as I lead with enthusiasm, confidence, and friendliness.

Throw Your Heart Over the Bar 40

...And your body will follow!

A famous trapeze artist had been instructing his students on how to perform on the high trapeze bar. After spending many hours lecturing them on the many intricacies of this skill, he requested that each one come forth to demonstrate his or her ability. One of the students became overwhelmed with fear as he gazed up at the insecure perch from which he was to perform. He completely froze in terror, with the horrendous vision of himself plunging to the ground. His muscles were paralyzed from fright.

"I can't do it! I can't do it!" he gasped. The instructor put his arm around the young man's shoulders and in a reassuring tone told him, "Son, you *can* do it! And I will tell you how." He said, "Throw your heart over the bar and your body will follow."

Courage is seeing your fear in a realistic perspective, defining it, considering alternatives, and then choosing to perform in spite of the risks. Effective leaders possess the courage and the desire to hurl themselves into those tasks that need to be done, whether they are pleasant or not.

A small amount of ability and a lot of desire will go a long way. The achievement of your goal is assured the moment you commit yourself and throw your heart into it. **If you have the heart, you have the power to attain anything!**

Application

As a leader, you will be challenged to take some risks. Prepare yourself to the best of your ability. And in those moments when fear has an overwhelming grip, burst out with fiery passion and throw your heart over the bar.

Tom Massey

When leading a team, create a daunting challenge or a noble mission that causes each team member to catch fire. One of the reasons group goals fail is they lack superordinateness—a theme so monumental that all members are compelled to perform beyond the ordinary. Teams that are intensely focused on such endeavors of passion work less for external perks, like money or prestige, than for the inner rewards of doing something inspiring that they love.

Affirmation

I am motivated by intense passion as I lead others to boldly throw their heart into what they do.

Unstring Your Bow 41

Re-create for success!

*T*he Greek historian Herodotus recorded a brief, yet telling story about King Amasis, who ruled in the Twenty-sixth Dynasty of Egypt from 570 to 526 B.C. Amasis had a daily routine of working diligently from dawn until noon, at which time he would abruptly quit whatever meetings or court proceedings were going on and retire for an afternoon of leisure. He and his companions told stories, played games, traded witticisms, and indulged in the "free-flowing barley ale." According to Herodotus, royal decorum wasn't a high priority in the afternoon activities of Amasis and his friends.

One day the advisors to the king reported to him that some people looked unfavorably on his afternoon routine. These folks, his advisors intimated, thought a king ought to act more dignified, in a "kingly" manner so to speak—one that befitted someone of royal stature. The king listened attentively as the advisors pleaded their case, and then responded, "When an archer goes into battle, he strings his bow until it is taut. When the shooting is over, he unstrings it again. If he didn't unstring it, the bow would lose its snap, and would be no good to him when he needed it in battle."

Herodotus said very little else about the king, except that Amasis was the most prosperous leader in the history of Egypt. Rest and relaxation are key ingredients for success. Too much work, with too little recovery time, can be overwhelming. As the tempo, complexity, and demands of work escalate, downtime should be increased to offset the overload of stress.

Effective leaders take regular time out from their rigorous schedules to recharge their batteries. They understand the importance of personal restoration. **Build time into your work schedule for re-creation activities to keep the snap in your bow.**

Application

How are you at unstringing your bow on a regular basis? If you were arrested for being good to yourself, would there be enough evidence to convict you? Create time in your schedule to relax. Go to a movie. Read a novel. Slip away for a fishing trip, a round of golf, or a weekend interlude with your mate, family, or friends. As you build a balance of leisure and relaxation into your life, you'll notice a livelier spring in your step and more snap in your bow.

As a leader, encourage the people who work for you to indulge in self-care, as well. By doing so, you will help them increase job performance and enthusiasm, while decreasing risks of job burnout. Be aware of symptoms of burnout in constituents, such as apathy, negativity, or exhaustion, and take precautionary actions by awarding time off for mental and physical health.

Affirmation

I ensure that I receive adequate amounts of rest and leisure time to stay mentally and physically sharp, and I encourage others to do likewise.

Use Every Setback 42

...As a positive motivator!

Three years out of high school, I became the epitome of the out-of-shape couch potato. I had grown up participating in sports, but settled into a sedentary life after graduation. My lifestyle and eating habits were unhealthy, to say the least. My idea of a seven-course meal was a hotdog and a six-pack of beer. I watched my waistline balloon from 28 to 42 inches in the few short years after I graduated.

An awakening came one night when I went out with a young woman named Cindy. She was an acquaintance from school that I had run into at a party. I asked if she would like to go to a movie and she consented, but I'm not really sure why. While on our date, she laughed at me and made cruel comments about my weight. She poked her finger into the spare tire around my waist and taunted me by calling me "Chubby." When I attempted to give her a goodnight kiss at the door, she turned her head.

The humiliation cut deeply, but it turned out to be a tremendous motivator. When I got home that night, I looked at myself in the mirror and swore that no one would ever make fun of me again because I was fat. I started doing push-ups and sit-ups that night, before going to bed, and began a strict diet the next day. I started running almost daily, which resulted in a loss of 75 pounds and 12 inches from my waistline over the next six months. My determination didn't stop there. As I began to get in better shape physically, I felt more compelled to work on mental fitness as well. I started going to college and eventually earned four degrees.

Everyone who dumps on us is not our enemy. Cindy performed a great favor for me. Her honesty, though a little brutal, was a wake-up call. Better her rejection, than heart disease or cancer in years to come because of an unhealthy lifestyle and obesity. Incidentally, I ran into Cindy a few

Tom Massey

years later in a grocery store. She looked like she had gained most of the weight I lost . . . but I didn't rub it in. Instead I thanked her for having such a positive impact on my life.

Effective leaders use every setback as an opportunity to "raise the bar" of performance in their lives. They look for the positive, with a willingness to learn and grow from each situation. **When life deals you a setback, rise up and use it to your advantage!**

Application

What setbacks are you facing? Is life unpredictable, or what? Just about the time you think you have it figured out, someone throws a monkey wrench into the gears. When that happens you have choices as to how you will respond. You can sit around, wringing your hands and fretting. Or you can bounce back with optimism and determination, searching for the proverbial pony in the pile of manure.

As a leader you have the opportunity to model self-control and motivation. Inspire others to rise above adversity. Lead by example and influence. When life smacks you up-side the head, learn from it. Be willing to alter your game plan and play smarter. Solicit feedback and engage others to help make that happen, as you build your organization's bridges to success.

Affirmation

I use every setback as a positive motivator and lead by example.

Vary Your Leadership Style 43

One size doesn't fit all!

*T*odd was bright, enthusiastic, and responsible. Although he had no experience, I hired him to manage a retail business, based on his great potential. From the beginning, I told him that I had confidence in his ability and offered full support for his decisions about the daily operations. But I remained a hands-off manager, offering little or no direction.

Within a short time, I noticed that his enthusiasm began to wane—and so did the profits. I stopped by occasionally and gave him a pep talk, assuring him he had my full support. But this had little effect, as the business continued to spiral downward. Soon he began to avoid making eye contact with me when I came into the store, and I began to second-guess my decision to hire him. Maybe he couldn't handle the responsibility after all, I thought.

After a little less than a year, we both became highly dissatisfied. He wasn't happy with the job, and I wasn't happy with the way he was performing. We finally reached a mutual decision to part ways. He left the business with strained feelings.

In retrospect, I can't blame him. I take responsibility for this unfortunate situation. I set Todd up for failure from the beginning by not giving him the direction he needed to manage the business. When I looked at him, all I saw was his potential, thinking, "If I can give him enough support and keep him motivated, he will be successful."

Effective leaders vary their leadership style based on people's *current* development needs. They *do not* manage in terms of potential, intelligence, or past successes. They *do* manage for competence, which is a demonstrated skill to perform a specific task. If a person does not have the competence to perform the task, all the support in the world will not make him successful. He must first receive direction in order to gain the know-how to do the job. Once his level of competence is sufficiently established, you may decrease directing and assume a more supportive role. **Effective leadership is always situational; one style doesn't fit all!**

Application

Are you flexible enough to vary your leadership style to develop both competence and commitment in people? Do you know when to use a directive style, or a supportive style, or a combination of both?

The first step is to stop and think before you act. Look at the situation and assess the development needs of others before deciding on the appropriate leadership style. Consider the following points when assessing development needs:

1. Identify the specific task and the knowledge required to complete it.
2. Determine the individual's current competence level for the task: Does she have the skills to perform the task with the desired outcome? Does she have transferable skills upon which to build new competencies quickly?
3. Determine level of commitment: Is he motivated? Is he confident?

For individuals who possess low levels of task competence, apply a directive leadership style, which involves: setting goals and expectations; showing or telling them what, when, and how to do the task; closely monitoring and evaluating their performance. For individuals who possess high competence, but low commitment, apply a supportive leadership style, which includes: soliciting two-way communication and feedback; providing encouragement; involving them in the decision-making process; promoting self-management. For some individuals, it is best to use a combination of directive and supportive leadership.

You may find that levels of competence or commitment fluctuate, especially as tasks and work environments change. Always adapt your leadership style based on development needs in the current situation.

Affirmation

I vary my leadership style according to levels of competency and commitment in the current situation.

Visionary Leadership

Elevate your mind above what you see!

*O*ne day a man was walking along the beach when he noticed a figure in the distance. As he moved closer, he realized the figure was that of an old man carefully picking something up and gently tossing it into the ocean. Approaching the old fellow, he asked, "What are you doing?" The man replied, "Throwing this starfish back into the ocean. It washed up on the beach last night during high tide and was left stranded."

The old man went on to explain that he walked the beach every morning, when the sun came up and the tide was going out, picking up starfish and tossing them back to safety. He explained that if he didn't, they would die.

"Sir, " the man said, "don't you realize there are miles and miles of beach and thousands of starfish? You can't possibly make a difference, you know."

After listening politely, the old man bent down and gingerly picked up another starfish. He carefully tossed it into the surf, then smiled and replied, "I made a difference for that one."

Most of us have heard this story more than once, but every time it is retold, a chord of inspiration resonates through our being. Effective leaders elevate their minds above what they see. Regardless of how insurmountable or daunting the situation may seem, they see beyond it and focus on what they can do to be a difference-maker. Like the starfish thrower, they believe that they can make a difference. When others become overwhelmed and are tempted to give up, **effective leaders stay the course, focusing on one starfish at a time.**

Application

Are you a difference-maker? Do you elevate your mind above what you see? Maybe you have become discouraged by a situation that appears to be too enormous to do anything about. If so, take a step back. Pay attention to what you can do to make a difference. Look at the big picture, but focus on the individuals whose lives you touch each day. Remember—a few simple acts, motivated by empathy and kindness, just might be the most important thing you can do today. Quantity makes the papers, while quality makes a difference.

Affirmation

I am a visionary leader and difference-maker as I focus on ways to impact individuals within my organization.

Who before What 45

Move from good to *great!*

*W*hen David Maxwell took over the helm as CEO of Fannie Mae in the early 1980s, the company was losing a million dollars every business day. The board desperately wanted to know what Maxwell was going to do to rescue their sinking company. Maxwell responded by telling them the correct first question should be "who," not "what." They had to get the right people on the bus before they could decide where it was going.

Maxwell began by telling his management team that there would only be seats on the bus for people who were totally committed to the success of the company. He met with every member of the team, informing them that the trip would be demanding and that he expected nothing less than top performance from each. He told them if they didn't want to go under those circumstances, "the time to get off is now—with no questions asked." Out of twenty-six executives, twelve stayed on board the bus, and Maxwell replaced the others with some of the brightest, most hard-working executives in the financial world.

With the "who" question answered, Maxwell turned his full attention to the "what" question. His management team took Fannie Mae from losing a million a day to earning over four million a day in less than a decade. And they generated cumulative stock returns that were eight times higher than the general market from 1984 to 1999.

Effective leaders understand that in order to move from good to great performances, they must answer the "who" question before addressing "what" or "where." They put the right people in the right positions first, and then focus on moving in the right direction. **Great organizations thrive because of the presence of great people!**

Application

Have you surrounded yourself with great people? It will be to your and your organization's benefit to do so. First, great people are self-starters who stay motivated to perform at high levels. They take pride in excellence. When they become part of a team of other motivated people, the results are astonishing. Great people are also flexible and adaptable to the changing business climate. They are not threatened when someone "moves the organizational cheese." When the going gets tough, great people get on the move. They rebound and respond quickly to take advantage of windows of opportunity that are continually opening.

When you put together a team of self-motivated people with clarity about the organizational mission and a high standard of performance, success will be the result. Make your number-one priority to hire the best people you can to fill the seats on your bus. Choose the right people *first*, and then choose the direction you want to go.

Affirmation

I surround myself with self-motivated and brilliant people who are building a great organization.

Write It Down 46

...And go public!

*T*wo prominent psychologists conducted a study on how human behavior is affected by public commitments. The basic procedure was to have a group of college students make a simple observation about some data they were given and derive a judgment based on their observation. Next, a sample group of one-third of the students was asked to commit themselves publicly to their initial judgments by writing them down, signing their names to them, and turning them in to the experimenter. Another third was asked to commit themselves to their initial judgments by writing them down, but privately on a Magic Writing Pad. Afterward they erased them by lifting the Magic Pad's plastic cover before anyone else could see what they had written. The third group simply made their judgments mentally, without writing them or telling anyone.

What the researchers wanted to find out was which of the three types of students would be most inclined to stick with their first judgments after receiving information that those judgments might be incorrect. So all of the students were given new evidence suggesting that their initial estimates might be wrong, and all were given the chance to change their decisions.

The results were conclusive. The students who had not written down their first conclusions were the least loyal to their original choices. When the new evidence was presented, these students were the most influenced by new information that could change what they viewed as the "correct" decision. Compared to these uncommitted students, those who had merely written their decisions for a moment on a Magic Pad were much less willing to change their minds when given the chance. Even though these students committed themselves under the most anonymous of circumstances, the act of writing down their decisions caused them to stubbornly resist changing their minds. But the researchers found that, by far, it was the students who had publicly recorded their initial judgments who most adamantly refused to shift from those positions later. Public commitment had solidified them into the most immovable of all.

Enormously successful companies have hit upon this simple method to inspire their staffs toward greater and greater accomplishments. When people are asked to set individual goals, then personally record them on paper and make them public, they create an unwavering commitment to the successful completion of those goals. **Effective leaders know that writing is believing!**

Application

First, write down the goals that you personally want to accomplish in the next year. Then share them with someone whom you trust and respect, to receive feedback and establish personal accountability. Next, ask your constituents to record their goals and share them with you. Offer encouragement, feedback, and collaboration if needed, and set up regular meetings to evaluate progress. Success breeds success! As people experience the fulfillment of their goals, they will become more confident and capable of scaling greater heights.

Affirmation

I ensure success and lead by example in writing and publicly acknowledging my goals and intentions of accomplishment.

eXcellence

The search continues

In Search of Excellence was on the *New York Times* bestseller list over three years and sold more than three million copies. In this highly acclaimed book on management and leadership, authors Tom Peters and Bob Waterman laid out the attributes they believed to be associated with excellent companies. At the time it was written, almost twenty years ago, the book received little attention in the world of business because the United States was experiencing serious financial distractions, with inflation hovering at 10%, prime interest rates climbing to 20%, and Japan eating America's lunch in the marketplace.

Peters admitted that he and Waterman were incredibly naïve, yet bold, when they first began doing the research for the book. They were looking at the world's largest companies and asking simple, direct questions, like: "Why do you do it this way?" "Why do you keep stumbling over your own bureaucratic feet?" "Why do you make it so hard for people to do their job?"

These questions came from one who, by his own admission, was "genuinely, deeply, sincerely, and passionately pissed off." Peters had been a student of Douglas McGregor, who invented Theory X and Theory Y, which proclaimed that people are an important part of business and they can't be motivated by controlling and tyrannizing. He said his frustration stemmed from his perception that "all managers in corporate America knew this was true, yet many, if not most, continued to treat their workers like s____!"

On reflecting back, Peters states that there was an almost Zen-like quality to their success. They were able to do it because they weren't trying to do it. In fact, he makes the point that "when it comes to managing and controlling people, only by not trying do you succeed."

Tom Massey

Effective leaders take this simple approach to management. They value the "real" people in the organization, those with dirty fingernails. Instead of obsessing over factors such as competitive advantage, economic growth, market dominance, or maximized shareholder value, these leaders pay attention to people. They are pivotal in creating a user-friendly, dynamically growing workplace where people become fully engaged, stay motivated, and learn new technology at accelerated rates. **The search continues . . .**

Application

Are you fully committed to excellence as a leader? Is your focus on numbers or people? It is understandable that turning a profit is important to you. It is a sign that the customer values the goods or services you produce. But the measurement of excellence is more than the profit line. It is about the heroic act of people throwing themselves on the line, in selfless pursuit of an ideal they believe in.

Listening to people is the key to building alliances. You may not agree with their ideas or use them, but there is always something to be learned. Be willing to break out of the "that's the way we do things around here" mold and experiment outside convention. Allow people the freedom to try new things. This will liberate their thinking, helping them to become smarter faster, in a world dominated by rapid changes brought about by the information-technology revolution.

Affirmation

I value the "real" people in the organization and create an environment for growth.

eXpect Delayed Gratification

48

Good things come to those who wait!

A missionary couple was returning home to America after devoting nearly twenty-five years of their lives to ministry in Southeast Asia. As their plane rolled onto the tarmac at the airport gate, they could see a crowd of people gathered with signs. Assuming that the crowd was there for them, the man commented to his wife that it was good to have such a welcoming reception to come home to.

After deboarding the plane, they discovered that the crowd was oblivious to their presence. Instead, the group had gathered to welcome a local music celebrity returning home from a concert tour. The man was openly disappointed and distraught that no one was there for them. "After all," he complained to his wife, "we have spent our lives ministering to people. Doesn't anyone care?"

His disappointment lingered. Within a few short weeks he began to become depressed and questioned whether God or anyone else cared about their years of service. His wife tried to cheer him up, but nothing seemed to be effective in pulling him out of this terrible funk. One day, feeling at the end of his rope, the man told his wife that he was going into the bedroom to pray about this situation. He was going to confront God once and for all as to why no one was there to welcome or acknowledge them when they returned home. He vowed to remain in that place until he received an answer.

The man spent the entire day in the bedroom with the door closed. His wife was becoming a little concerned when he finally emerged from the room. His countenance had noticeably changed and he appeared to be in a more peaceful state. His wife asked whether he had received an answer, and he nodded.

Tom Massey

"What was the answer?" she asked.

He replied, "We're not home yet."

Effective leaders have a certain spiritual quality. They are able to delay gratification for the short-term in exchange for fulfillment of a long-term vision. Leadership can seem like a thankless task. Sometimes we don't reap the rewards or see the effects of our actions for years. **When you don't see quick results, you can choose to become disgruntled, or to patiently trust that your actions have a significant purpose.**

Application

Which do you focus on more as a leader—success or significance? Success-driven leaders focus mainly on results. Their passion lies in getting tasks done right, accomplishing goals, and recording quantifiable results—all of which are admirable goals, but often narrowly focused on short-term achievement.

Leaders who rise to levels of significance are able to let go of their attachment to short-term results and move purposefully toward the realization of their long-term vision. They focus on doing the right things, as much as doing things right. And they understand that the quality of work is not always measured by public recognition or profits.

The key to your effectiveness as a leader is *balance*. Balance your drive for success with an aspiration for significance.

Affirmation

I lead with significance, as I stay focused on the fulfillment of my vision.

Yield the Power

Promote autonomous decision-making!

*C*indy is a property director for a residential management company. As a new year began, we were discussing goals and resolutions. I asked her what kind of work-related goals she had set for the upcoming year. She said that her boss, a corporate vice-president, had set all of her goals and informed her that she would be evaluated in relation to how twenty-five other property directors performed. There would be one bonus awarded to the person who turned in the most outstanding performance for the year.

I asked Cindy whether her boss had asked for her input when creating the goals or the criteria for measuring her performance levels. She answered, "No."

"Hmmm," I said. "How would you respond if your spouse walked in with a set of personal goals that *he* had written for you, and threw them down on the table saying, 'Here are your yearly goals, honey. I'll let you know at the end of the year how you measure up.'"

She replied that she would, in all probability, tell him where he could stick his goals. I chuckled because I know her well enough to know that would be the last time her spouse would make that mistake. I asked her how she could set such clear boundaries personally, but not professionally. She replied that she didn't really have a choice if she wanted to keep her job.

Cindy may not have a choice about accepting work-related goals from this autocratic boss, but she does have control over her own level of commitment. How loyal do you think she will be to those goals? How much ownership will she actually take? Not much, probably. Certainly less than she would have if she had been given some say-so in the matter.

Tom Massey

Effective leaders promote autonomy through collaborative decision-making. **The success of any corporate goal is determined by the commitment of the individuals who do the work.**

Application

Put yourself in Cindy's shoes. How would you feel if you were left out of the loop on decisions that affect you? This may be an effective style of leadership for soldiers going into battle, but it is not effective in the business world. Always include people in the decision loop when setting performance goals. Let the situation dictate how much or how little. If a person is relatively new on the job, with low levels of competency, then take a more dominant role in establishing objectives. If the person has extensive experience and high competency, then allow her the dominant role. Either way, make it a collaborative process.

Affirmation

I always include others in decision-making and goal-setting.

Your Hill To Die For?

50

How committed are you?

*T*he warriors in certain Native American tribes had an interesting battle tradition. When they reached a point of no retreat, they would
find an elevated place to make their stand. In that place, they would plant
their spear and tie one of their legs to it, refusing to give ground. Through
this act of courage and decisiveness, they served the world notice that this
had become their "hill to die for."

In these times of waning loyalty and rapid change, now more than ever,
it is essential for leaders to model unwavering commitment to stay the
course in the face of adversity. They must know that unrelenting people
have the power to change the world.

Like pebbles in a pond, effective leaders send ripples throughout an
organization. They possess the courage and dedication to stand behind
tough decisions regardless of how unpopular they may seem. An example
of this relentlessness can be seen in Lee Iacocca's decision to cut the wages
of the entire workforce rather than enact massive layoffs, in a heroic move
to save Chrysler Corporation during hard times. At the time, organized
labor groups were critical of his actions. Popular wisdom dictated that he
find another way to save Chrysler, but Iacocca knows that "popular wisdom" can be a contradictory term.

Those who are truly committed must be willing to make personal sac-
rifices for the larger, long-term good of the organization. They are the
"patriots" who rally group morale and confidence. **When the going gets
tough, effective leaders plant their spears in a determined effort to
make a lasting difference.**

Application

Have you found your hill to die for? Are you unyielding, optimistic, and action-oriented? The ultimate act of leadership responsibility may be in taking control of your own mind when your back is against the wall. How you respond to crisis will influence others. Prepare with the following steps:

1. Think about the positive things that you can accomplish in the current situation. Look for the silver lining in the cloud.
2. Allow yourself adequate time to prepare a constructive response to adversity.
3. Offer words of encouragement and optimism to coworkers and constituents.
4. Prepare for the worst, and expect the best. It's not what happens to you, but how you respond that counts.
5. Avoid perfectionism. Remember there is no such thing as failure—only outcomes.

Affirmation

I act with courage and commitment in times of adversity.

Zero In on Your Health

51

Create fiscal and physical fitness!

I lived and worked on a ranch in Oklahoma in the late 1970s. Jack Hall, the old fellow who owned the ranch, treated me like a son. I was an avid long-distance runner in those days, and each morning I would log between five and ten miles up and down the road that ran in front of the ranch. I really enjoyed those mornings of running the road as the sun came up, smelling the aroma of fresh cow manure on wet grass.

Practically every morning, Jack would sit and watch me run from his office, atop a hill overlooking the entire spread. At the time he was suffering from emphysema and lung cancer, so exercise for him was limited to an occasional walk around the barn.

One warm summer morning as I finished my run, Jack motioned for me to swing by his office. I stood there soaking wet from an exhilarating workout, feeling euphoric as runners often do. He looked at me wistfully, and his words are still etched in my mind. "Son, I'd trade everything I own for your youth and vigor," he said.

The saddest irony of life lies in the fact that "we don't miss the water until the well runs dry." Jack died less than a year later, but his words live on in my mind. Here was a man of vast wealth who would have willingly traded it all, just to feel good again physically. But unfortunately, when it comes to health, we often don't miss it until it's irretrievably gone.

Effective leaders do not take their health for granted. They understand the impact that a healthy diet, adequate sleep, and a regular exercise regimen have on their energy and ability to lead. Goals and business plans matter little to those who are sick. **For what should it profit you to gain the whole world, and lose your health?**

Application

Physical fitness can lead to increased fiscal fitness in a variety of ways. First, you will experience less down time because of sickness and poor stress recovery. You will also experience increases in energy and stamina, which will help you to work harder, with greater longevity. Brain functioning is enhanced, which leads to working smarter and more creatively. Self-confidence and self-esteem are also improved.

Use the following guidelines to create your physical fitness and personal health program:

1. **Diet**—Eat light, eat often, and eat a variety of foods. For peak performance, eat higher amounts of protein during the morning and afternoon, and high complex carbohydrates, such as pastas and vegetables, during the evening. Make the front line of your diet grains, fresh vegetables, and fruits, while staying away from high-fat, fried foods. Practice the 80/20 rule—80% of the time eat a balanced diet, allowing a 20% margin for lavish indulgence.

2. **Sleep**—This is your number-one stress recovery factor. The adequate amount of sleep for the average person is six to eight hours per night. Establish a routine of going to bed and rising around the same time each day.

3. **Exercise**—Make it fun and painless. A well-rounded exercise program should include aerobic activities, such as walking, jogging, biking, or swimming, three to four times per week. Perform light weight-lifting and stretching exercises two to three times a week to strengthen bones, muscles, and connective tissue.

Affirmation

Health and physical fitness take a high priority on my daily schedule as I create fiscal fitness through working smarter and living longer.

Zoom In 52

...On your part to play!

*T*here once were four people named Everybody, Somebody, Anybody, and Nobody. An important job had to be done and Everybody was sure that Somebody would do it. Anybody could have done it, but Nobody did it. Somebody got angry about that because it was Everybody's job. Everybody thought Anybody could do it and that Somebody would do it, but Nobody realized that Everybody thought Somebody would do it. It ended up that Everybody blamed Somebody when Nobody did what Anybody could have done.

Does this scenario sound familiar? Do the people in your organization depend on somebody to do the job that anybody can, yet nobody does it? It's time to take the bull by the horns, as my grandfather used to say. Make things happen. Become that somebody that gets everybody involved in getting the job done. As the Nike commercial says, "Just do it!"

Effective leaders are proactive. They lead with a sense of purpose, optimism, and self-guided determination, regularly stepping up to the plate in anticipation of hitting a homerun. **Your willingness to roll up your sleeves and actively participate will ultimately influence your effectiveness as a leader more than personality or intelligence.**

Application

Here's your chance to take action. Don't just finish this book and set it on the shelf, carving another notch in your intellectual belt. Apply the principles daily, along with the Four P's of Effective Leadership:

1. **Purpose**—Develop a statement of purpose that clearly defines *why* you are doing what you do. When people have a good reason to do something, they can overcome great odds to succeed.

2. **Picture**—Visualize what the outcome will look like *when* you successfully accomplish your purpose. Paint a mental picture for others so that they can share the vision.
3. **Plan**—Develop a strategy for *how* to achieve your purpose and make your picture of success a reality. Break the plan down into daily, weekly, and monthly goals that are quantifiable. Evaluate the progress of those goals regularly.
4. **Parts**—Decide *who* plays which part in implementing the plan. Each person on your team should know that every part is important. A chain is only as strong as its weakest link.

The Four P's cover the Why, What, How, and Who questions of effective leadership. The only question left is—When? The time to start is *now*. Just do it!

Affirmation

I put these words into practice, taking an active part in leadership and inspiring others to stay involved.

Books Available From Robert D. Reed Publishers

Please include payment with orders. Send indicated book/s to:

Name:_____

Address:_____

City:_____ State:_____ Zip:_____

Phone:(_____)_____ E-mail:_____

Titles and Authors	Unit Price
____ *Gotta Minute? The ABC's of Effective Leadership* by Tom Massey, Ph.D.	$9.95
____ *Gotta Minute? The ABC's of Successful Living* by Tom Massey, Ph.D., N.D.	9.95
____ *Gotta Minute? Practical Tips for Abundant Living: The ABC's of Total Health* by Tom Massey, Ph.D., N.D.	9.95
____ *Gotta Minute? How to Look & Feel Great!* by Marcia F. Kamph, M.S., D.C.	11.95
____ *Gotta Minute? Yoga for Health, Relaxation & Well-being* by Nirvair Singh Khalsa	9.95
____ *Gotta Minute? Ultimate Guide of One-Minute Workouts for Anyone, Anywhere, Anytime!* by Bonnie Nygard, M.Ed. & Bonnie Hopper, M.Ed.	9.95
____ *A Kid's Herb Book for Children of All Ages* by Lesley Tierra, Acupuncturist and Herbalist	19.95
____ *House Calls: How we can all heal the world one visit at a time* by Patch Adams, M.D.	11.95
____ *500 Tips for Coping with Chronic Illness* by Pamela D. Jacobs, M.A.	11.95

Enclose a copy of this order form with payment for books. Send to the address below. Shipping & handling: $2.50 for first book plus $1.00 for each additional book. California residents add 8.5% sales tax. We offer discounts for large orders.

Please make checks payable to: **Robert D. Reed Publishers.**
Total enclosed: $_____. See our website for more books!

Robert D. Reed Publishers
750 La Playa, Suite 647, San Francisco, CA 94121
Phone: 650-994-6570 • Fax: 650-994-6579
Email: 4bobreed@msn.com • www.rdrpublishers.com